*Making Sense of the
College Curriculum*

Making Sense of the College Curriculum

Faculty Stories of Change, Conflict, and Accommodation

Robert Zemsky,
Gregory R. Wegner,
and Ann J. Duffield

Rutgers University Press
New Brunswick, Camden, and Newark, New Jersey, and London

Library of Congress Cataloging-in-Publication Data

Names: Zemsky, Robert, 1940– author. | Wegner, Gregory R., 1950– author. |
Duffield, Ann J., 1947– author.
Title: Making sense of the college curriculum : faculty stories of change, conflict, and
accommodation / Robert Zemsky, Gregory R. Wegner, and Ann J. Duffield.
Description: New Brunswick, New Jersey : Rutgers University Press, [2018] |
Includes bibliographical references and index.
Identifiers: LCCN 2017053554 | ISBN 9780813595023 (cloth : alk. paper)
Subjects: LCSH: Education, Higher—Curricula—United States. | Education, Higher—
Aims and objectives—United States. | College teaching—United States.
Classification: LCC LB2361.5 .Z45 2018 | DDC 378.1/990973—dc23
LC record available at https://lccn.loc.gov/2017053554

A British Cataloging-in-Publication record
for this book is available from the British Library.

∞ The paper used in this publication meets the requirements
of the American National Standard for Information Sciences—
Permanence of Paper for Printed Library Materials, ANSI Z39.48-1992.

www.rutgersuniversitypress.org

Manufactured in the United States of America

Making Sense of the College Curriculum is dedicated to the 187 faculty members who shared their stories with us—without their candor and willingness to talk about their frustrations as well as their aspirations, there would have been no tale to tell.

Contents

Preface

An Exercise in Sensemaking

As a team, we have often worked together, mostly under the banner of the University of Pennsylvania's Institute for Research on Higher Education. Much of that effort involved special projects. First came the Pew Higher Education Roundtable with its principal publication, *Policy Perspectives*, and then its successor, the Knight Collaborative. We played central roles in two federal research and development centers—the National Center on the Educational Quality of the Workforce (EQW) and then the National Center for Postsecondary Improvement (NCPI), a Stanford partnership that included the University of Michigan and the University of Pennsylvania (Penn). Eventually our work came to center on helping individual colleges and universities, often serving as consultants supplied by the Learning Alliance for Higher Education.

We offer this recitation of bona fides as testimony to the fact that the "we" in the volume you have before you is not a ubiquitous "we" but rather just us—Ann, Bob, and Greg—not quite the three musketeers, but a team nonetheless that has drawn repeatedly on its collaborative work over the last thirty years. Each project has planted seeds that ultimately led to other explorations and publications. Our interest in curricular reform has two antecedents. In the early 1980s, Joseph Johnston of the Association of American Colleges (AAC) visited us at Penn to ask if the institute might be able to test statistically whether the American undergraduate curriculum lacked coherence as AAC's *Integrity in the College Curriculum* was about to report. We accepted AAC's invitation and eventually came to document just how right the authors of the AAC report were. We returned to the question of curricular coherence supported by a pair of grants from the Spencer and Teagle Foundations. The findings from those efforts became an integral part of Bob's argument in *Checklist for Change* that institutional efficiency was not possible without curricular efficiency. *Checklist* attracted a variety of interesting as well as interested commentators, including Judith Shapiro, former Bryn Mawr provost, former Barnard president, and by then, the newly installed president of the Teagle Foundation. She sent Bob the

kind of letter every author wants to receive—filled not with praise but agreement: "I especially appreciate the central role you give to the faculty in any
necessary and desirable change. It is indeed counterproductive to see them as
the enemy, unless we have a plan for making administrators and board members do all of the teaching. If we want to engage students, we need to engage
faculty members. And we need to have them function not just as a community
of scholars, but as a community of teachers."

Even more succinct was her concurrence with *Checklist*'s portrayal of
what passed for curricular revision on most campuses: "You are so right about
what the usual process of curriculum revision generally involves [logrolling
by both] faculty and students. . . . What are the hopes for something better?"

Our first answer to her question was a promise to document what worked
and what didn't work as colleges and universities struggled to revise their
curricula. We should have known better. It was a promise that couldn't be
kept, largely because there have been so few examples of curricular changes
that were truly ambitious. Four years later that original promise has morphed
into a restatement of the problem as a riddle that needs to be solved. Why
has there been so little curricular change? Why hasn't there been the same
kind of restructuring of university curricula in response to disruptive change
that has recast the work of lawyers, librarians, bankers, and even physicians
as their fields have changed? Through our conversation with Judith, we came
to understand that someone needed to talk with faculty, to listen to them,
not as adversaries or recalcitrant participants, but as actors in a drama with an
increasingly uncertain denouement.

On behalf of the Teagle Foundation, Judith asked and we gratefully
responded that we would indeed like to take on the challenge of talking with
and listening to faculty members across a wide spectrum of disciplines and
institutions. For this assignment we reached out to five colleagues that we had
met along the way: two English faculty members (Lisa MacFarlane and Jennifer Summit), one communications faculty member (Lori Carrell), one psy-
chologist (Susan Baldridge), and one expert on academic governance (Matt
Hartley). They were also experienced administrators who, having shepherded
reform efforts on their own campuses, knew how faculty talked and the kinds
of stories they were likely to tell. The other characteristic many of them
shared was that they had new jobs—Lori Carrell, over the course of the study,
went from being the faculty leader responsible for the University of Wiscon-
sin Oshkosh's new general education curriculum to being vice chancellor
for academic affairs and student development at the University of Minnesota
Rochester. Lisa MacFarlane went from being the provost at the University of
New Hampshire to serving as the principal of Phillips Exeter Academy. Jennifer Summit, who had led the transformation of the curriculum of the Stanford

English Department, now serves as the interim provost and vice president for academic affairs at San Francisco State University. Susan Baldridge, formerly dean of the faculty, next served as provost of Middlebury College. And Matt Hartley is now the associate dean of Penn's Graduate School of Education. Only the three of us—Ann, Bob, and Greg—did not change jobs, but then we had already spent more time on other people's campuses than on our own.

From the outset, we faced three challenges. The first was to develop a credible sample of institutions that would help us collect faculty stories. We did not want a random sample; rather, we wanted institutions that we knew had grappled with curricular change. We were remarkably lucky that all eleven institutions we invited to participate in our study agreed to do so. In all, we recruited four liberal arts colleges, including one highly selective institution; one new experimental public institution; one community college; three comprehensive institutions (two public and one private); and two major research universities, one a public flagship university and one a private, highly selective research icon.

Our second challenge was to enlist, within these eleven institutions, a reasonable sample of faculty members. In each case, the leadership of the participating institution selected the faculty, almost all of whom were either tenured or tenure eligible. We knew it would be easier to persuade faculty who were interested in curriculum reform to tell us their stories, so we urged our contacts on each campus to include a reasonable number of skeptics, individual faculty members who would be more likely to tell stories of missed opportunities and wrong-headed experiments. In the end, however, we recognized that what we had collected were the experiences and perspectives of faculty doers, those who had a sense of agency and a vision. These are faculty who are motivated to give back to the academy—a concept that is part and parcel of the idea of faculty having a calling.

It is important to note, as the consent form we asked each faculty storyteller to sign made clear, that we were recording conversations rather than conducting interviews. We had no standard battery of questions to be asked. Our interest in stories, as opposed to answers, stemmed from a conviction that good storytelling was, in fact, sensemaking—a story that makes sense is one that satisfactorily explains an experience, event, or idea. There is also the notion that faculty committed to changing their institutions are engaged in a process of collective sensemaking. Here there are echoes of faculty socialization and the profession's sense of how best to prepare faculty members for the work at hand. It is a notion that shapes a faculty member's self-concept while simultaneously shaping his or her view of the world.

Our third challenge was to find a way to explain why there has been so little curricular change—changes in how American colleges and universities educate their undergraduates. What we had collected was a treasure trove of faculty stories full of opinions, concerns, and consternations: 187 recorded faculty conversations in all, yielding more than 7,200 typed pages. We envied Studs Terkel, kept a copy of his *Working* close at hand, and actually thought about producing a volume like his full of stories and with minimal commentary. But we also understood that most of our stories, no matter how good they were, could not stand on their own—as Terkel's stories mostly did.

When faculty talk about the curriculum, they talk about it as a thing. Ideally, a curriculum gives expression to the ideals, values, and goals of the academy and of the individual disciplines it comprises. But a curriculum is also an organization of people and tasks that seeks to represent an academic perspective in a practical way. Not surprising, then, most curricula are negotiated arrangements often achieved through well-established governance and political processes—hence the need to include a substantial amount of interpretative discourse explaining the context of the stories we had collected while in parallel explaining first the importance of each story and second how each one helped answer the questions that had launched our study in the first place.

The solution is a text that is story rich in that roughly half of the words come directly from our conversations with the faculty. We have interwoven full-bodied, Studs Terkel–like stories throughout the pages that follow. All our stories are offered anonymously, except on occasion, where we identify the storyteller's discipline and broadly describe his or her institution.

First came the recorded conversations stored as encrypted MP3 files. Next, the separate sessions were transcribed. Each transcript was read at least by one or, more often, by all three of us. We prepared summaries of each session, noting what was (and occasionally, what was not) interesting about the recorded conversation. Ultimately, this process of reading and rereading the transcripts produced a catalog of interesting stories—one with many more entries than there was room to include in this volume.

At this point, we became not just collectors of stories but editors as well. We needed to help make our stories readable while remaining faithful to the storytellers' voices. We eliminated typical and distracting patterns of human speech: "you knows," "ums," "ands," and "likes." In order to facilitate the understanding of a story, we deleted storyteller thoughts that interrupted the plotline. All care was taken to retain the storytellers' speech rhythms and cadences, their own metaphors, references, and jokes. Alas, words didn't always convey the gesticulations that most good storytellers use to emphasize portions of their tales, so we might not always have fully conveyed their motions and even their emotions. During editing, words and phrases were occasionally inserted to clarify the flow of a story or to re-create how much passion the storyteller felt, although this was rarely necessary, since their stories tended to reveal even more than was probably intended.

Books about higher education typically include the collection and analysis of numeric and related data to support the conclusions they share with their readers. This quantitative approach is usually considered to be "real" research in the minds of most faculty, administrators, and board members. This volume will likely disappoint some, in that our conclusions are not based on numbers and other forms of hard data, but rather on stories.

Storytelling of the kind that we have drawn upon for this volume preceded the collection of data and related evidence by at least three thousand years. In 1845, Austen Henry Layard, Henry Rawlinson, and Hormuzd Rassam recovered from the ruins of Mesopotamian palaces thousands of stone fragments, which ultimately were pieced together into twelve ancient tablets. Eventually they were stored in the basement of the British Museum, where George Smith, an English archaeologist, discovered them in 1872 and set about translating what came to be known as the eleventh tablet of the *Epic of Gilgamesh*.

Smith's work in turn became the subject of a 2014 article in *The Atlantic*, "The Psychological Comforts of Storytelling," by Cody C. Delistraty, which related how the eleventh tablet tells the story of "a character named Utanaphishtim [who is] told by the Sumerian god Enki to abandon his worldly possessions and build a boat. He is told to bring his wife, his family, the craftsmen in his village, baby animals, and foodstuffs. It is almost the same story as Noah's Ark, as told in both the Book of Genesis and in the Quran's Suran 71." The question Delistraty ultimately addressed was "Why start telling stories in the first place?"

> Their usefulness in understanding others is one reason, but another theory is that storytelling could be an evolutionary mechanism that helped keep our ancestors alive. The theory is that if I tell you a story about how to survive, you'll be more likely to actually survive than if I just get you facts. For instance, if I were to say, "There's an animal near that tree, so don't go over there," it would not be as effective as if I were to tell you, "My cousin was eaten by a malicious, scary creature that lurks around that tree, so don't go over there." A narrative works off of both data and emotions, which is significantly more effective in engaging a listener than data alone. In fact, Jennifer Aaker, a professor of marketing at the Stanford Graduate School of Business, says that people remember information when it is weaved into narratives "up to 22 times more than facts alone." (Delistraty 2014)

The stories we have made the subject of this book were told by faculty members who believe passionately in teaching and learning. Many of them also fear that attacks on higher education—its cost and its value—will ultimately erode public credibility in and support of their institutions. Many of these stories are indeed about survival. Our hope is that our presenting of these stories will enhance their capacity to provide the kind of evolutionary mechanisms that will help keep their colleges and universities thriving.

Given the monumental nature of the task of conducting 187 separate story-collecting sessions, the multiple reading of more than 7,200 pages of transcriptions several times, and the constructing of a text that broke many of the rules of expository writing, our debts to friends and colleagues are substantial. Our first acknowledgment is due to the members of the story-collecting team—Jennifer, Lisa, Lori, Matt, and Susan—who joined us as we traversed the continent and helped us make sense of what the transcripts revealed. Judith Shapiro and Loni Bordoloi Pazich, on behalf of the Teagle Foundation, contributed to both our methodology and our findings. Madeleine Green, a friend and colleague of long standing, sat with us as an inside-outside critic as we put together this volume's final text. Among her many contributions was her insistence that the final text reflect the larger meanings embedded in our stories. Given our promise of anonymity, we are more indebted than we can properly acknowledge to the presidents of the eleven institutions we visited and to the senior staff members who organized our story-collecting sessions on their campuses.

One of the real miracle workers in this process was Pat Frazier, who was responsible for transcribing each of the recorded conversations. On average, each of the transcripts ran to forty typed pages or more. Rick Morgan was responsible for the in-house editing of our manuscript. He also made sure that our editing of the transcriptions followed the rules we had laid out for that task. Pam Erney was the project manager and majordomo, who moved us around the country, coordinated with each campus's designated representative, and generally smoothed the feathers that we inevitably ruffled. Kimberly Guinta of Rutgers University Press took on the task of gently guiding us as we experimented with a variety of ways to present the faculty stories we had collected. Scribe Inc. was responsible for the final copyediting and more than honored our sense that the faculty stories were not imbedded quotations but rather integral parts of the text.

Our largest debt is to the faculty who shared their stories with us. They know the answer to the riddle we posed, but they also know that they alone cannot solve it. Their energy and passion have made the telling of their stories a true pleasure. For all these reasons and more, this volume is dedicated to them.

Robert Zemsky
Gregory R. Wegner
Ann J. Duffield
Summer 2017

*Making Sense of the
College Curriculum*

PART ONE

 Defining the Task

Introduction

FIRST CAME *A Nation at Risk*—an unexpectedly harsh indictment of what many had accepted as a national strength. The words didn't just sting; they inflamed, helping ignite an educational reform movement that thirty years on has yet to run its course: "We report to the American people that while we can take justifiable pride in what our schools and colleges have historically accomplished and contributed to the United States and the well-being of its people, the educational foundations of our society are presently being eroded by a rising tide of mediocrity that threatens our very future as a Nation and a people. What was unimaginable a generation ago has begun to occur—others are matching and surpassing our educational attainments" (National Commission on Excellence in Education 1983, 1). Most of higher education, however, just shrugged off the critique, assuming that the real target had been K–12 education in general and the nation's failing high schools in particular. That was in 1983.

Two years later, the Association of American Colleges (AAC) released *Integrity in the College Curriculum*, the product of a select committee largely drawn from the ranks of higher education and those institutions committed to the liberal arts. Among the notables who worked on the project were Arthur Levine, David Breneman, Robert McCabe, Gresham Riley, and Martha Church. Williams College's Fred Rudolph was generally credited with the drafting of the report. The text began modestly enough, noting that in 1982 when they began their work, *Integrity*'s authors understood they "had joined a chorus." There was, however, nothing quiet or choral-like about what followed—indeed, in tone and style, *Integrity* simply outdid *A Nation at Risk* in calling out the nation's colleges and universities for being satisfied with what had become a shopworn product. The chapter addressing the issue of the status of the baccalaureate degree was pointedly titled, "The Decline and Devaluation of the Undergraduate Degree." Nothing escaped the select committee's barbs: "The business community complains of difficulty in recruiting literate college graduates. Remedial programs, designed to compensate for lack of skill in using the English language, abound in the colleges and corporate world. Writing as an undergraduate experience, as an exploration of both communication and style, is widely neglected. College grades have gone up, even as Scholastic Aptitude Tests and American College Testing scores have gone down and the pressures on teachers to ease their students' paths to graduate schools have increased" (AAC 1985, 1).

The committee saved its harshest criticism for the college curriculum itself:

> As for what passes as a college curriculum, almost anything goes. We have reached the point at which we are more confident about the length of a college education than its contents and purpose. The undergraduate major . . . in most colleges is little more than a gathering of courses taken in one department, lacking structure and depth, as is often the case in the humanities and social sciences, or emphasizing content to the neglect of the essential style of inquiry on which the content is based, as is too frequently true in the natural and physical sciences. The absence of a rationale for the major becomes transparent in college catalogs where the essential message embedded in the fancy prose is: pick eight of the following. And "the following" might literally be over a hundred courses, all served up as equals.

What caused this state of affairs? "The curriculum has given way to a marketplace philosophy: it is a supermarket where students are shoppers and professors are merchants of learning. Fads and fashions, the demands of popularity and success, enter where wisdom and experience should prevail. Does it make sense for a college to offer a thousand courses to a student who will only take 36?" (AAC 1985, 2).

While there was plenty of blame to go around for the nation's curricular foibles, the authors of *Integrity* were particularly unhappy with their faculty colleagues: "The development that overwhelmed the old curriculum and changed the entire nature of higher education was the transformation of the professors from teachers concerned with the characters and minds of their students to professionals, scholars with Ph.D. degrees with an allegiance to academic disciplines stronger than their commitment to teaching or to the life of the institutions where they are employed" (AAC 1985, 6).

Eventually AAC itself began to worry whether its select committee, having laid out their displeasures for all to see, had somehow missed the mark. It was at this point that AAC's Joseph Johnston came to visit Penn's Institute for Research on Higher Education (IRHE) to ask whether the institute might be able to calibrate and then verify *Integrity*'s conclusion, "As for what passes as a college curriculum, almost anything goes." We could, we said, provided AAC supplied the funding and helped the institute get access to the undergraduate transcripts needed to test whether undergraduate curricula, because they had fewer requirements and less course sequencing than before, were yielding educational programs that lacked curricular coherence. What we found, more than thirty years ago, was as dismaying as it was baffling. It was true. Undergraduate curricula in almost every kind of college and university were being "destructured," just as the authors of *Integrity* had charged. Anything and everything was possible. There was neither coherence nor much rigor reflected in the transcripts analyzed. Along the way we spoke with a faculty member who told us he assumed that in each class he taught, regardless of its numbering or presumed place in the curriculum, almost every student enrolled in the course had little or no prior understanding of his field's basic precepts. Outside of the sciences, there were few truly introductory classes—freshman and sophomores were as likely to be sitting next to juniors and seniors as to students like themselves, who in the past would clearly be recognized as beginners. Nor could the IRHE staff find a curriculum that was anything but a list of courses that satisfied some set of often-murky requirements.

The larger disappointment, however, was the fact that neither *Integrity*'s critique nor the IRHE's analysis led to any noticeable change in what was happening to college curricula. The report was celebrated and quoted. The institute's analytic team was congratulated on the cleverness of its statistical routines. Across the higher education landscape, individual faculty were intrigued, but not enough to forge a new consensus requiring a more structured or a more coherent undergraduate curriculum. The faculty had learned, only too well, the pleasure of allowing each instructor to do his or her own thing. Reinstituting requirements would have made faculty responsible for what their students took with them into the next set of courses in an ordered and sequenced curriculum.

It would be wrong, however, to assume nothing changed because of the critiques offered by *A Nation at Risk* and *Integrity in the College Curriculum*. Quite the contrary—what ensued was a truly remarkable reform movement that focused not on the curriculum but on pedagogy. Fixing the problems identified by the critics, it was argued, required a fundamentally different approach to teaching and learning, one that produced an engaged student learner. Again, it was the Association of American Colleges, newly rebranded as the Association of American Colleges and Universities (AAC&U), that took the lead. Year by year, conference by conference, publication by publication, AAC&U laid out an agenda of high-impact practices that framed the pathway to a more engaged student learner. In 2005, AAC&U expanded its call for a broad-based educational reform by launching Liberal Education and America's Promise (LEAP), a national public advocacy and campus action initiative designed to focus renewed attention on liberal learning in general and liberal arts colleges and universities in particular.

At roughly the same time, the Pew Charitable Trusts provided the funding necessary to create the National Survey of Student Engagement

(NSSE). Largely based on the work of Peter Ewell and Russell Edgerton, the NSSE assumed that while it was still not possible to measure the student outcomes of individual institutions directly, it was possible to estimate an institution's likely success by noting whether its practices promoted student engagement. For nearly twenty years now, NSSE has tracked changing institutional practices, noting when and where individual institutions seemed to be making unique contributions to higher education's learning enterprise. But like AAC&U's efforts, questions of curricular structure and coherence received little if any attention. What mattered most was how individual subjects were taught, not how they were linked together in particular curricular patterns. The one exception was the AAC&U's focus on general education, where, in fact, it argued that what was required was more than a smorgasbord of introductory courses. The larger impact, however, was a torrent of interesting experimentation—new courses, new subjects, new ways to integrate in-class and out-of-class experiences. Students often responded by pursuing double majors, added internships, and new ways to make the old seem new by combining it with something different. The result was curricula that made little if any pretense of offering either structure or coherence to the undergraduate learning experience.

Such was the state of affairs when Harvard's Derek Bok gently called to task the enterprise he had spent a lifetime shepherding through good times and bad. The former president's *Our Underachieving Colleges* tells much the same tale *Integrity* had told twenty years earlier, though certainly Bok's friendly critique and even the title of his book were much easier to swallow. But Bok's critique is important, not just because of who he is and was, but because he wrote about how higher education had a largely unfinished agenda: "The good news is that most of the serious deficiencies can be overcome, at least to a significant degree, given the will to do so. The bad news is that most of the problems are not being seriously addressed on campuses today, nor will they be until they are correctly identified and clearly understood by those responsible for the quality of teaching and learning in our colleges" (Bok 2008, 10). The problems Bok identified were the same as identified by *Integrity*: too much unconstrained student choice, too little understanding of what students ought to be learning and the skills they ought to be acquiring, and too much acquiescence in a faculty culture that fits faculty interests but not student needs:

> The second persistent problem in the work of the faculties arises from the traditional independence of professors and their departments. In most colleges, debates over the curriculum are not a means of imposing order but a process for reaching a consensus among autonomous scholars. By

common consent, no tenured professor should be forced to do anything. Very rarely is a department compelled to assume teaching responsibilities against its will. When the majority votes for specific requirements, it is often assumed that the necessary courses will all be staffed voluntarily, even if it means that someone must be found to teach them. (Bok 2008, 39)

And it turns out, as more and more institutions are learning to their chagrin, unfettered faculty independence combined with unfettered student choice is simply not economically sustainable. Not surprisingly, then, just two critiques dominate public discussions of higher education today. First, American colleges are too expensive, in large part because they lack the will and the know how to do things differently. And second, far too many students start but do not finish their baccalaureate educations.

Initially it was thought that these two concerns—escalating costs and disappointing attainment rates—were separate problems, a division of responsibility as well as blame that mirrored higher education's view of itself as having a hard side where monies are concerned and a softer "more nurturing side" when helping students achieve their academic ambitions. There is, however, a perfectly straightforward linking of these two observations—one that challenges collegiate faculties to reshape their undergraduate curricula, making them more efficient both in terms of learning and costs. Curricula that are overly complex or overly filled with requirements whose principal logic is the preservation of faculty positions cost both students and faculty time and money—or as a host of students at one public comprehensive proclaimed when asked to evaluate the institution's general education curriculum, "It's a waste of my time and my money." Some of the students' comments were wonderfully prescient in their estimate of the faculty's commitment to a well-formed introduction to the liberal arts. As one student put it, too much of general education does nothing "more than keep particularly irrelevant courses funded and tired faculty continually employed." The third most common complaint was that the faculty did not understand the requirements, which helped explain why advising too often left students taking the wrong road to graduation (Zemsky 2013, 149–150). Instead of fixing the problem, however, most faculties have left in place smorgasbord curricula whose principal purposes are the protection of disciplinary agenda, the faculty's interest in teaching what they feel most comfortable teaching, and their students' pursuit of curricula that allow them to choose among a wide variety of courses every time they register for a new semester. It is as if the way to run an upscale restaurant is to allow every customer to define his or her own menu and the chefs in the kitchen to cook only what they want to cook.

It was but a short step to extend this argument, as was done in *Checklist for Change*, offering a pair of axioms for guiding the kind of reform that is now necessary. The first held that "higher education is the faculty's business." It is what faculty do and take responsibility for that will matter most. The faculty's teaching and explorations will depend on the academy's continuing commitment to the scholarship of learning and discovery. Achieving that future as opposed to one of diminished faculty roles will require forceful but, more important, collective action on the faculty's part. As individuals, faculty members will have to abandon that sense of themselves as independent actors and agents. The financial crisis of the new century has taught everyone that talking about "my money" or "my students" or even "my research" brings few benefits and no friends. Faculty need to be frank about the need to share the money—and will have to understand that they neither own nor possess their students, though, as faculty, they have an important responsibility to ensure their successful learning.

Checklist for Change's second axiom held that the change that is needed most is curricular change. A substantial portion of the increase in operating expenses at most colleges and universities derives from the "faculty collectively teaching (and often requiring) more subjects but individually teaching fewer courses than before." It is the propensity problem—"the irresistible urge to add new subjects reflecting the ever-expanding nature of the knowledge base while almost never deciding *not* to teach something else." Majors expand, double majors proliferate, internships become ever more important, yielding graduating transcripts more likely to record 140 credits or more rather than the standard 120 units students would earn if they took five three-unit courses per semester for four years. In many institutions, the propensity problem "increases the probability of more under-enrolled classes. Often the pool of students pursuing a specific major or specialization has, through the continuing addition of new and advanced courses the faculty want to teach, been divided and then divided again until at any given moment only a handful of students are available to take a given course at a given time" (Zemsky 2013, 182).

Why has there not been more curricular change of the kind called for by the authors of *Integrity in the College Curriculum*? That is the question—the nub of the riddle that is the subject of the volume you are about to read. If you want to see if we actually solved our riddle, we invite you to skip to "Conclusions," where we present, in summary form, our answer. We hope, however, that you will not do that, choosing instead to work through the parts en route to a better understanding of the whole. We hope you will proceed as we in fact did, starting with an understanding of the passions that motivate faculty, the singularity they vest in their own autonomy, and the frustrations they encounter when seeking to bend their institutions to their will. Any understanding of what it means to be a faculty member—scholar, teacher, guide, interpreter—and hence a potential agent of change necessarily requires first an appreciation of the passion most faculty bring to their calling and second an awareness of how faculty connect with their students. Despite the parodies that cast us as muddle headed and confused, we are usually almost embarrassingly explicit about what motivates us—it is what often makes us intellectual absolutists. Nor, as it turns out, are we impervious to change. One of the themes common to almost all our faculty stories is an awareness that both teachers and students have changed and, in fact, are continuing to change.

We have also come to understand how the principles that animate the faculty find their way into the curriculum. Just as important are those topics faculty have trouble talking about—race and politics and the dwindling support they receive from the public at large. No less important is the need to understand how instructional faculty are coming to terms with the need to teach differently, teach more collaboratively, and teach better using social media and other new technologies.

With those experiences and predilections as a foundation, we knew we needed to explore how faculty identify, to themselves and to their colleagues, the specific obstacles to curricular reform. The first, not surprisingly, was the sheer difficulty of eliminating anything—courses, majors, minors. The curriculum and its options may be constantly expanding, but time, as the faculty know only too well, is a finite resource. Money is the second finite resource—and what is most unnerving of all is just how often faculty see themselves engaged in processes that never seem to end. Too often it is a matter of being told, "Sorry, but you can't get there from here."

Our hope is that you will come away with the feeling that you have been invited to witness real faculty conversations that were mostly unguarded and, for that reason, remarkably revealing. We start off with an illustrative story from a physics professor that captures the kinds of uncertainty often reflected in how faculty talked about what did and did not work as they went about the business of changing how and what they taught. The organization of the volume consists of five parts. Following this introductory part is the second part called "Passions," which features stories and commentary reflecting the passions that send faculty into the classroom—what motivates them and why. We present two perspectives here: the sense often expressed by individual faculty that they are bridges enabling their students to learn, on the one hand, and to cross over those bridges and grow from their experiences, on the other. The next chapter and accompanying longer stories focus on "why faculty do what they do." We thought it important to begin with a portrayal of the things that make faculty special—as both teachers and as learners—as an antidote to the cynicism that is coming to characterize public characterizations of the academy and its faculty denizens.

The next part focuses on the adaptations faculty have made to changes in their own lives as well as those of their students. It has become all too easy to portray faculty as being resistant to change—and that is just not the case. Like members of learned professions everywhere, faculty have had to make substantial adjustments in both their definitions of acceptable practice and in their expectations defining acceptable outcomes. It is those accommodations that have often shaped the kinds of changes faculty are prepared to make in both what and how they teach.

Making Sense of the College Curriculum's fourth part—"Frustrations"— explores the particular obstacles that confront faculty seeking to change the curriculum. Some of those obstacles involve a paucity of money. Others derive from the rules the faculty themselves have put in place to preserve their independence. Still others reflect an overelaborated bureaucracy that too often has a mind of its own.

Our concluding part offers our solution to the riddle we have posed, describing in Frostian terms, "The Road Not Taken."

One last piece of unsolicited advice. You might well consider reading the stories themselves out loud so that, quite literally, you come to hear the faculty voices we have collected. That said, our hope is that you will solve our riddle on your own—and that you too will come to understand just why *Integrity in the College Curriculum*'s call for college curricula that are more purposeful—as well as more coherent—has yet to be answered.

Faculty Voice

HARD CONVERSATIONS

The following story is from a full professor who is a member of her college's Educational Policy Committee.

A lot of distrust built up between the faculty and the administration over some of the decisions that were being made about where the college was going in terms of expanding our base. That affected all of the conversations that were taking place on campus. Committees representing the faculty, such as the Educational Policy Committee or the Faculty Council, struggled to have conversations that didn't feel like they were just part of an exercise. Faculty weren't sure whether there was already an end game planned out by the administration, and that made it difficult over those years to have what I really felt would be meaningful change at the institution. That isn't to say that meaningful change didn't take place, but those conversations were always fraught.

Over the last couple of years, one of the things that happened was the initiation of a very broad discussion about restructuring faculty governance. We now have a new model that we're following, and as I think back over how this occurred, the board of trustees was restructuring, and so I think it made sense for faculty to restructure at the same time. But the aim of the process was amazing because the whole idea was to try to find structure. I think part of it was that our faculty meetings were more and more poorly attended and the conversations just didn't seem to be that useful. We found ourselves arguing about some little, tiny phrase that was in some piece of legislation instead of talking about the substance of legislation. So some of our wise elders (I'll refer to them as such) were involved in this process of thinking about how we could alter what we were doing in such a way that we could get back to a place where we really could have meaningful conversations and where we could get input from junior faculty members instead of the same cast of characters. You could sort of predict who was going to stand up and make comments about various things, and it was really difficult to get broad input from across the campus.

Plenary meetings with organized discussion groups in between were one element of a broader restructuring. We also now have two new faculty committees. One of them is supposed to be very creative without thinking about resources or the implications of cost but looking five to ten years out. The other is a group of faculty representatives that are meeting with the trustees on a more regular basis and thinking about what's best for the institution from a faculty viewpoint. The chair of the board is trying to break down those old walls and get us to have the kinds of conversations where trustees and faculty are not talking past each other.

This whole process is a very good idea and will facilitate the role of the Educational Policy Committee. Right now, the Educational Policy Committee wears two hats. One is staffing. If departments need to fill some sort of staffing hole in the department, they submit a proposal, and this particular committee puts it forward. Our other responsibility is for curricular change, and in both roles, we tend to be reactive rather than proactive. Somebody sees there's something that they want to do differently, and they'll propose something to this committee rather than the committee saying we're going to be proactive on a whole bunch of different things.

Here's the current process. When an initiative or proposal to do with curriculum comes forward to the Educational Policy Committee, we follow the process in our faculty handbook. We typically vet the proposal by having some conversations with the individual or individuals who bring the idea forward and with various other constituencies. We then pull together language for a piece of legislation. Depending upon how significant the change is, I think we're required actually to have two open faculty meetings after we propose some piece of legislation to the faculty. We make some changes and iterations and then bring it back to the faculty again. That's sort of the standard route.

If we have to consider a bigger curricular change, then we'll have perhaps a survey of the faculty in the spring of one year and say we're going to look through the responses that we've gotten. In the following fall, we bring the ideas together and move forward some legislation to the faculty. There is more discussion and more iteration. So it can be a really long process, and sometimes that drives people nuts. But it gives everyone an opportunity to have their voices heard, and it gives the committee an opportunity to make changes. You never get it right the first time, and people help us try to fine-tune or alter what we're doing.

I think that having organized faculty discussion groups as part of the new process is going to be so essential—getting faculty members together in a room and hearing why one faculty member is so angry about not doing blah and having the other people hear that and be able to respond to it in real time instead of only at a faculty meeting. I've seen on several occasions the pathology that happened under our old system. A piece of legislation would come before the faculty. Those open meetings had happened, but people were busy and didn't really have a chance to go to them (which is why I think these smaller group meetings between these plenary sessions are so important), then you got to the plenary meeting and somebody—usually with good intentions—would propose something as an amendment, and the legislation just would go off in some completely different direction. This pathology has happened on several occasions in the last ten to fifteen years. Maybe the new governance structure will curtail this behavior and also balance out our committee's role of being a reactive body.

I'm thinking about the fact that it's always a struggle to know what the right balance is between courses that are just for the major—higher-level, upper-level courses—versus some of those really broad introductory courses that are definitely really important for the institution. There's been a little bit more of a push from faculty in recent years, when we feel as though we're under a crunch, to say, "OK, we're not going to do that general introductory course" or "We're not going to do this specialized seminar for first-year students that we should be doing." These are conversations that are hard to have, and I want over the next couple of years to keep reminding people in gentle ways and not sort of hitting them over the head—although maybe I need to do that—that we are part of this institution.

PART TWO

 Passions

CHAPTER 1

I Am a Bridge

SHE WAS A TRIPLE returner to the Midwestern University at which she was now a faculty member. She had started the university twice as a student, first as a freshman who took two courses and then left, terrified. "I'm from town, right? I'm a townie, and I was not prepared at all to come to college. I didn't have parental support; I didn't have a lot of things that we assume that a student might have." Then she came back as a single mom with a toddler. Even then she was like everybody else, a learner who didn't know why she had to do what she was being made to do. "I mean, I'm the original 'Why am I taking all of these classes that make absolutely no sense to me?'" And then she came back a third time, now as a faculty member knowing well her calling:

> I always tell my students, "Your brain is a lot more like Shakespeare's brain than mine is because you live at this time of rapid change, just rapid change." And they are so creative. They do things with the stuff they find on the internet and together, we just can't keep up with it. But what they miss is that there's depth there; they miss that there's a story there because they're young people and they have no sense of history. They don't understand. We need to help them understand how this is part of something bigger to which they belong and for which they will be responsible.
>
> So I always say my growth as an individual scholar and a person, a creative person, is I'm a bridge. I'm trying to help these people to understand what's important and what we can't lose like the fool who says, "I don't know what's going on; I'm going to fall right off the edge."

Those four words—"I am a bridge"—succinctly capture the story we want to tell about the passions of faculty members who teach. Teaching itself is a profession that calls upon its practitioners to reach beyond their own needs and concerns, to act on the potential exhibited by students who seek to expand their prospects through education. Faculty members of the universities and colleges we met are bridges in the sense of connecting students to skills and knowledge traditions, thus contributing to the development of thinking and attributes of character that their students will ideally carry with them throughout their lives.

The persona of a teacher in the public mind is not always flattering. Teaching is not the highest-paid profession, and that fact in itself makes it susceptible to a certain amount of ironic treatment. In literature and popular culture, the stereotypical image is often of one who is not well suited to other occupations in life—"those who can't do, teach."

Today, virtually every college's and university's marketing materials proclaim the value placed on quality teaching. For all that, within the culture of many colleges and universities, there is an ambivalence toward faculty members who make the teaching of students the principal emphasis of their careers. Faculty members by and large were trained in a single academic discipline, and for tenure-line faculty in most baccalaureate institutions, the highest standard of achievement is research and publication in a peer-reviewed journal or monograph. Many have remarked the disparity between the professional and financial rewards accorded to research achievement on the one hand and quality teaching on the other. While it is important to teach well, for tenure and promotion, published research and peer acclaim remain the gold standards for advancement in a traditional faculty career. In some institutions, the organizational structure and language of support for faculty delineate between "faculty development," referring to research support, and "teaching."

Nonetheless, the most basic finding from our conversations with faculty over the course of two years was the vitality of these scholars' commitment to teaching itself. Regardless of institutional type or the expectation of research as part of a faculty member's responsibilities, the faculty we met consistently voiced the centrality of teaching as a primary element of their professional identity, as well as a source of personal satisfaction. In describing the value of what they do as teachers, faculty spoke consistently of their students' learning in terms that extended beyond the course itself or the field of study in which they themselves were trained. No one offered a rendering of the dismissive claim that "I teach chemistry, not students." With the exception of those preparing their majors for certification in a service profession, virtually no one described their immutable goals for students as creating the next generation of research scholar-practitioners in their discipline.

Instead, those who spoke to us about teaching described the broader educational benefits they hoped their students would gain—from the institution as a whole as well as from their own courses. Nearly all of them exemplified the fundamental claim that "I am a bridge"—helping create passageways or traversing impediments for students, helping connect them to sources of development and growth in knowledge, capacities, and self-discovery. Far more than infusing their students with the content and methods of a given discipline, their passion for teaching stemmed from their success in helping students make connections with the potential they saw in their own lives. Again and again, faculty described the fulfillment that results from helping students discover that learning is a passion, a skill, an identity, even a calling for something they had not known in themselves.

COMMITMENT TO STUDENTS

A commitment to the educational success and well-being of students was a theme voiced repeatedly by faculty members across our sample of institutions. Common to all remarks was the conviction that students were, to a considerable degree, the faculty's raison d'être. One of the most spirited declarations of commitment to a student's success is from a setting in which such commitment is a hallmark of the institution's culture:

> This institution has a long tradition of being passionate about its students. I felt that when I came here. The faculty that mentored me in my job were people that would drop everything for a student. They just would. And I realized that I had been very fortunate that this was the job I had because that's what I wanted. I wanted to be in a place where I can drop everything because a student's at my door. I don't need to close my door because I have to get some other work done. My work is that student knocking at the door. During my impressionable years here, I heard more and more stories about how Professor M. knew just what to say to get a student who was struggling to get back on task and Professor C. would go over to a student's house who hadn't been showing up at class. These [were] remarkable stories. I realized over time that being a professor wasn't saying the right words so the student could understand it; it was a deeper human behavior that people in positions of responsibility share with those that they're trying to mentor. So I have tried to carry on that tradition. The younger faculty, one in particular in my department, speaks with me in these same tones that I used to speak with Professors M., C., and L. You can see it chokes me up that he thinks that I'm like that because I felt I had a responsibility to become that kind of person here.

As we traveled from campus to campus, we were struck again by the extensive range of people who are included in the term "student body." Traditional-aged undergraduates seeking a residential learning experience constitute a large part of this population, though for many decades, the number of students seeking higher education in other modes, other social and financial circumstances, and other seasons of life has equaled or surpassed the number of rite-of-passage undergraduates. For institutions that serve students for whom education is one of several concurrent life challenges, it is not uncommon for a faculty member to take on the role of informal counselor on matters beyond the classroom. Even on campuses that are residential learning communities and have invested substantially in student support programs, faculty members find themselves reaching out to students who experience learning challenges stemming from events in their lives. A faculty member's commitment to students comes to mean more and different things than was common three decades ago:

> We're in an underprivileged part of town, and I have a lot of students who have issues that are not academic. A lot of our students are working multiple jobs; a lot of them are caring for their own kids; they're caring for parents; and they're caring for family members. They're really stretched, and sometimes life takes them out and they'll withdraw from their class. Those are the students who I really can't pull back, even though I might reach out to them. I tell my students at the very beginning of semester, "There's no prize for getting there first, but there is a prize for getting there. If you have to stop out, make sure you come back. Don't just walk away." I try to reach out to them when I see they're starting to not come regularly and say, "What's going on?" We have an early alert program where counseling will call them. We have a student success coach who unfortunately was funded by an external grant. Her position is going away, and she's fantastic. She would reach out to them and coordinate resources for them. That intrusive advising is critical with this population of students. It's not a silver bullet and one-size-fits-all. It's throw everything you've got at it. That's really the only way we're going to make progress. I have forty-five-year-old grandmas taking care of their grandkids. I have kids with incarcerated parents. You name it, it's there. I give them a lot of credit for showing up every morning.

INHERENT CAPACITIES

One of the too often uncelebrated skills that derives from a commitment to their students' success is the ability of faculty members to discern qualities that students themselves may not know they possess. In that sense faculty are guides helping surmount perceived obstacles, drawing out the potential that students exhibit and taking deep satisfaction in bringing to fruition the seeds of talent within those they teach:

> Our community center, which has been on campus for forty-five years, is living, breathing civic engagement. This is probably the most creative part of my teaching, because you're taking students through the transforming experience of providing legal assistance to the community. I've got a student now who's graduating. She was in my general ed. class four

years ago. When she got up to do her presentation then, she couldn't stop shaking. She wouldn't look out at the audience, and she was sweating so badly. Everybody in the classroom felt bad for her. She's now a director for an environmental advocacy program, and I saw her about a month ago make a presentation before probably one hundred people, and—it gives me chills—she had this clear voice and an articulate, powerful presentation. Being able to see this change coming out of a little program that runs on a shoestring was mind-boggling. Afterwards, I just gave her a hug, and I said, "I am so proud of you pushing yourself." And she said, "You all gave me the vehicle by which to do that." And that reward to me trumps everything.

Some faculty describe their teaching as an act that goes beyond the discovery of talent to helping students discover an identity—to learn who they are and what they are capable of doing in their lives:

> Students have to learn to be uncomfortable with having some ideas that are, "Oh, it's not quite it." They have to iterate and fail and come back to it, and that's hard for people to do. I'm really interested in asking, "Who does the student get to be here? What is their identity? Can they be a historian? Can they be a scientist? Who do they get to be in this space (especially if we want them to stay in our fields)?" Students have to be able to see their identity here. "I'm the kind of person who does these things." I think that shift in identity is important, and when I butt heads with colleagues in productive ways, it is because we really think differently about learning and how people learn to do something.

Teaching beyond the Disciplines

One finding from our conversations was a notable counter to the frequent image of faculty members having a foremost allegiance to their own expertise. The familiar critique of faculty as being more concerned with their disciplines than with their home institution and students was certainly present in our conversations, though it was not the single or even predominant theme. While there are some who gauge their achievement by the number of majors who proceed to graduate or professional study at a major research university, virtually everyone in a faculty career understands that the metric of his or her own effectiveness extends beyond that criterion. Many voice an awareness that not all students they teach will major in the subject, much less proceed to advanced study. In most cases the motivation for teaching well is not self-replication as scholars or investigators in the field. It is instead to contribute to students' development by providing them with tools from the faculty member's discipline that can apply to other areas of knowledge—and other aspects of students' lives. A recurrent theme from our stories was the potential of imparting transferable skills from the study of a given field:

> I personally have said and believe that if a professor can show that they are meeting the outcome, then it doesn't make any difference what the prefix is to that class—if it's accounting, if it's sports administration, if it's English. All of those have equal rights to delivering outcomes in creativity. I came to the realization of that in a sort of backward way. I was never very good at history until I went to college and learned music history. It was very interesting to me that I could understand history through music. If we were looking at the French Revolution and the American Revolution and the reduced power of kings, I understood that best by looking at the music of Beethoven. Beethoven was writing for larger symphonies because his audience was getting larger because the people were coming to hear the symphonies instead of music being performed just for the kings. So to allow people to explore creativity through their major enables them to work with what they already own.

In another story, a math professor tells of a student who learns a core skill in a topic of study. What is interesting in this case is that the teller conveys a dual perspective on what a student has learned. There is both a sense of satisfaction at the thought that the student will excel in a career that draws from the subject of study and an affirmation that the essential skill learned in this context—to recognize patterns rather than memorize formulas—will confer a benefit in contexts beyond the discipline itself:

> I had a student who was in this introductory algebra class three semesters ago, and he was one of the few students who seemed to understand the higher-level modeling with different types of functions we were doing in that class. That's a college algebra class. That's the first math class that actually would transfer to university. He did well with that and now he's taking Calc II. You have to have that function concept down in order for any of that analysis to make any sense to you. And he started out in developmental math. He's going to be an engineer. And it's like "Whoa!" A lot of his success is due to his own drive and his own motivation, but I do think his understanding of the function concept has been a key piece in his progress. There are a lot of those functions in that introductory math sequence that if students stumble over them, they give them problems for the next three or four semesters. You see them in calculus class struggling with the same thing. I tell my students, "Math isn't so much about memorizing formulas. If you're memorizing stuff, you're doing it the wrong way. You want to be able to re-create it." It's more about seeing

patterns, and it's more about a way of thinking. It's funny because, believe it or not, sometimes the best students in the class are the ones who are the artists. Patterns. They see the patterns, and that's really what it is. "Don't memorize stuff; just see the patterns."

The accounts of faculty who were also visual artists describe how they have encouraged students to reach beyond a level of ability that comes readily to hand and to explore what is possible by applying a different lens to a subject and creating meaning that expresses a way of seeing. Stories of this kind convey something more than teaching students a technique in a particular set of parameters; within the specific context the faculty member describes, the vignettes express the goal of instilling ways of seeing and thinking that lead students to an enhanced understanding:

> We're finding that there are a number of students that come to us who have strong skill sets in drawing, and they think, "If I can draw photographically, that's the pinnacle. That's what I should do. And if I can already do that, why would I do something different?" So we do a lot of work in trying to say, "OK, if you draw photographically, wonderful. Anything set in front of you, you can document. What's the character of that drawing compared to one where you've had far too much coffee? You can't do a straight line. Careful."

> I have a project called "The Caffeinated Drawing," and the intention is to stress thinking, to look at the character of the mark, not how photographic it is. You can still create the illusion of three-dimensional space, and it is only an illusion. Or you can still do that with scribble kinds of marks and students find that awkward. And I say, "But it's about the character; it's not about necessarily the accuracy. This is one more way of describing or thinking about that form."

HEIGHTENED PERSPECTIVE

A feeling of satisfaction often derives from the sense of helping students understand the learning process itself—and their own learning—from a heightened perspective. A challenge that faculty members often encounter is the need to help students recognize that their frustrations about learning may stem from the ways in which they study and approach the task. It is not uncommon for students to employ ineffective study methods that have been developed and solidified from earlier schooling. At times, then, the goal is helping students examine their own learning practices and ask whether their accustomed approach is the most effective. There are accounts of faculty members acting as bridges to help their students achieve a distance—to stand apart from themselves, in effect—and to view critically the way they process information. Helping students think about their thinking, to learn from their successes and failures, is central to what several faculty describe:

> I have a lot of students who are very good thinkers and they are good at problem solving. They may not recognize that they're good at critical thinking, but they are and they understand that better when they know what metacognition is. I have lots of athletes in class, and after I tell them what metacognition is, I give them an example. "What do you do after every game?" "Oh, we watch a film of it." "What do you do when you watch the film?" "Well, we go back and we look at what we did, where we made our mistakes." And I say, "Don't you also look at what you did well so you can reinforce that? And then look at what you did wrong so you can correct it?" I've always talked about ethics, but I teach process for critical thinking. I don't just teach content. We think a lot, and they're not going to get through my course if they don't think. I'm against memorization and regurgitation.

By whatever name, the act of helping students see their own learning process from an enhanced critical perspective becomes, for many faculty members, one of the most important contributions they make to their students' learning and development:

> We include what's called "metacognition" in our rubrics, and metacognition is "thinking about thinking." We ask students to reflect on their own thought process and to become aware of that process. This helps them to develop the process itself. As they become more "metacognitively aware," their memory improves. When we talk about critical thinking or creativity or something that's really challenging, some students do it naturally and others struggle with it. When we ask them to become metacognitively aware of their own thought process as they think critically or creatively, they begin to understand how they personally think. My students in my learning and memory course had to write an entire page of their paper on the creative process that went into each of their projects. I had a set of questions designed to get them to think about, "How do we create things? How did you come up with your idea in this project? How did you solve the problem? What things jumped out at you that helped you to create what you did?" I got some fascinating answers that demonstrated that students had started to become aware of how they think creatively.

Another mark of this principle is the value some faculty members attach to helping students look beyond the facts themselves and ask the question that makes possible a deeper inquiry into the issues being examined. The skill of asking the salient question, which opens passages to new thinking and understanding, is among the greatest gifts a teacher can bestow on a student:

> One idea that has come about is we have students taking all these courses across six different learning perspectives. Right now, there's nothing that makes sense of these learning perspectives other than the discipline you're taking. We call them learning perspectives and students go, "Hum?" And then they say, "I'm taking a history class." So about a year and a half ago, the [planning group] thought, "What if we took these six learning perspectives and oriented all the courses in each perspective around what we'll call a 'signature question'? What's the signature question of the historical approach? What's the signature question of the social science approach?" The idea is that a student ten years after college, when thinking about problems, might remember two or three of these signature questions and just use them every day as a part of how they relate to the world.
>
> The idea came to me actually when I got this award a couple of years ago and, shoot, seventy-five of my former students wrote me when they heard about it. It was amazing. And every one of them told me the thing they remembered from my class. I wish everybody could have that experience. You get it at your funeral, but by then it's too late. Anyway, one student, a vice president in a bank in San Francisco, said, "When I'm in meetings, people at my work know I'm the one in the room who always asks the question that is the game changer. That's what people rely on me to do and that's what my role is. We talk and talk, and then I ask a question, and we go in a different direction." And she says, "I learned in your classes that the best approach to life isn't knowing stuff always but being able to frame the right question." That meant a lot to me because teaching students how to ask good questions is a big emphasis in my courses.

No one can miss the sense of vocation expressed in that testimony—the fulfillment of purpose that comes from having imparted tools of thinking and expression that help students be effective in their lives.

Role-Playing and Enactment

When assistant professors talk candidly about the review process for tenure, it is not uncommon to hear about the anxieties that surround the evaluation of teaching. Often the story goes like this: "I had my students in three small groups one day, each working to frame an argument for the topic that they would debate in the last half hour. Then in walks the division chair unannounced and tells me he is here to observe my class. The student groups continue talking and working together. Five minutes later the chair gets up to leave and tells me, 'I'll come back another day, when I can see you teach.'"

"When I can see you teach." The little phrase embodies a deeply rooted conception that defines teaching as the act of delivering knowledge to students and learning as a student's accurate recounting of that content. Notwithstanding what research has taught about how learning occurs, the premise remains that a teacher's role is to deliver authoritative knowledge, and a command of a subject is the only thing needed to teach.

Yet many faculty members with whom we spoke described effective teaching practices in ways that differ from the role of teaching as talking. To be certain, no one has wholly abandoned the practice of lecturing to students; when it is carefully structured and aptly timed, addressing students in a lecture can be an enormously valuable way to enhance knowledge and understanding. But our narratives made clear that faculty members employ a range of methods that offer pathways to learning for their students. The pathway sometimes consists of creating the context in which students engage with one another or with people and events sometimes extending beyond the classroom itself.

One of the methods that can increase the opportunities for learning is to assign roles to students for dramatic enactments of a scenario, sometimes drawn from historical events. Asking students to take on another identity based on their understanding of a significant historical moment can lead to perspectives beyond what might have occurred in the classroom context alone. In some cases, role-playing can help students increase their skill in speaking a second language while increasing their historical understanding:

> For language classrooms, I think we have always been on the cusp of putting students at the center of the experience. I mean we tried to de-emphasize our place at the front of the classroom as much as possible and have devised all kinds of strategies for making sure that students are in control in the classroom. They're practicing; they're practicing; they're leading; they're talking. So we have de-emphasized the lecture model over the years. If I'm teaching, for example, a play and I can get students to actually dramatize that play, even a few scenes, that's wonderful. Last year my students put on an entire medieval farce for the campus at large. The place was packed, and they were doing it in French. The whole thing was in French. I mean, there's a big classroom down the hall, and it was absolutely packed. It got really hot in there.
>
> When I do the revolution in my civilization course, I have a day where I have the "beheaded return." So these students go out and do all this research, and then they come back impersonating those revolutionaries

that they have studied. They get angry with each other and they say, "And you! Louis XIV! You did such and such and such and such." I think it makes it more relevant for them when they can actually embody those kinds of roles, so there's a lot of dramatization and playacting that goes on. I think modern language pedagogy has changed a lot from when I was a student and mostly read and analyzed the text for its literary value. There is a place for that, and we do that, but I've moved largely away from that because like I said, I try to find things that are more relevant to them and how they're going to use the language.

Faculty who create scenarios for dramatic enactment recognize that this process draws upon inherent skills that students in many cases have not had occasion to apply. In preparing their students to perform in a context that is defined but ultimately unscripted, an instructor invests students with confidence in their ability to apply their knowledge and the techniques of communication they have practiced. The following instance makes clear that in addition to affirming the students' own potential to succeed, role-playing can also help allay doubts that others, including faculty colleagues, express about their own students' ability to succeed in an applied learning context. The exercise becomes a teaching moment for everyone involved:

> I'd helped put together with some chancellor's office monies a town hall for the community focused on homelessness, and the assistant city manager really liked it. He took me to lunch and said, "I think we need something to improve civil discourse in city council meetings, and I wonder if you think you could do anything about that." The more we talked, the clearer it was that he would like some rules of discourse, like maybe a debate. So I said, "Well, you know we have this communications studies department on our campus, so let's sit down at a table with some of them." I arranged for that, and then a couple of amazing faculty members, the city manager, and I developed something that we called the "Great Debate." That's become our largest event. The students take over the city buildings for that. They take over city council and city hall, the old municipal building, the big outdoor city plaza. It grew from three hundred students to six hundred to two thousand because the local community college bought in.
>
> It was with the Great Debate that I started to think that the provost who thought I should work with faculty wasn't crazy after all, because I always had to talk the faculty off the ledge the night before the big events. They'd say, "My students aren't ready; we can't do it." And then I'd say, "No, it's going to be OK; they're going to rise to the occasion." The students would and then the faculty would weep. They'd see their

students in these public spaces facilitating discussions, giving a panel presentation, or engaging in dialogue, and it would just do them in. It was really something.

Dramatic enactment and role-playing, combined with analysis and discussion as pedagogical techniques, can also be powerful elements in the development of affective qualities in students. In this instance, the faculty role is once again to create the context in a course that gives rise to learning in students. The insight revealed in this vignette derives from what students themselves have done in the learning space created through role-playing, and the lesson derived registers with greater impact than either a textbook or lecture, in itself, could impart:

> Applied theater is a very powerful tool. The workshops I'm doing now are called "Difficult Conversations in a Clinical Setting." I had the students come in and partner up with another person, and first they had to think about a clinical experience where they had encountered or experienced a difficult conversation either as a patient, as an intern, or as someone who had been shadowing a practitioner. I didn't frame it any further than that. I just said, "It's up to you to define what that means to you." They had to be very confidential and were asked not to name facilities or individuals. I said, "You have to figure out a way to be able to tell that story in thirty seconds to your partner; it has to have a very clear beginning, middle, and end." So they sat down and wrote out and then told each other their stories.
>
> We then said, "Now you have to come up with an image using both of you, and you can bring in a third person if you want." I had my student assistants there. This image is a snapshot of the moment when it shows that this was a difficult conversation, and so they came up with these images. We call that "Image Theater." We then showed them to the rest of the group and just froze them at that moment. We didn't have any dialogue. We didn't introduce anything. We said, "What do you see here? Let's just throw out words." People would throw out words like, "fear," "distrust," "disengagement," "sadness," whatever it was. Usually the image is so powerful that there's no doubt that something is not going well. Somebody had one person with their back turned and the other person pointing and trying to talk at them. Another person had the patient very clearly looking up, wanting connection to the practitioner, but the practitioner was looking down and writing in a notebook. Or the practitioner towering over the person who's sitting down—those kinds of things. We put up all the words on a board and talked about them and the things that we got from them.

At the next level, we added one or two lines of dialogue to the scenes. They did that to give a little bit more framing to it. Sometimes the dialogue was, "I'm really scared of what you just told me," and then the practitioner says, "Oh, you'll be OK, and here's your prescription." This built a little bit more of a picture around the scenes.

We took our lunch break, and everybody talked about it, and then we said, "OK, so now what we're going to do is we're going to find the moment where it became a difficult conversation. And now you get to 'utopianize' it." I'm going to probably change that word, because I ended up saying, "I don't want you to make it unbelievable, but I want you to show how the script can be switched so that it ended up being a better experience for the practitioner and/or the patient." And they did really well. They built these really incredible scenes where you could see the moment, usually when the patient or the other person in the scene asks for something, and the practitioner has a choice at that moment. They all had the practitioner being responsive, not towering over them but getting down on their level, just really simple things.

At the end, we talked about these scenes, and they came up with this incredible list of takeaways. One of the things that I thought was really powerful was when one of them said, "Empathy can be learned." That was great because I want them to know that these are skills. You're not born with them, but even as an adult, you can learn these things.

Experiential Learning

A next step in support of student learning that leads beyond the classroom is to invite students into the realm of direct engagement with others in actual life. The faculty member who encourages students to interact with people—neighbors and citizens—outside their academic setting helps construct bridges to learning that can have powerful, even transformative impacts on the students' development.

Some of the stories we collected make plain the benefit that can result from augmenting traditional class instruction with lived experience. For a faculty member who seeks to prepare a next generation of leaders to become stewards of the nation's natural resources, the value of supplementing reading and instruction with direct experience of nature is indisputable:

I do a fair amount of agency training and a lot of project-based strategic planning for most of the federal resource agencies, so that has provided an interesting opportunity for our students as well as for the agencies, because part of what I bring to an agency partner is a millennial perspective. Our university's entrance sign makes a commitment to a better tomorrow, which makes it fairly easy to talk to agencies and colleagues about, "If you want tomorrow's traveler today, they are here. If you want tomorrow's manager today, they are here. If you want tomorrow's executive today, they are here."

In this state, we have this remarkable system of publicly supported campuses, which is an astonishing force for good if we ever seriously leverage our system. I had the greatest fortune of being able to provide lots of students with free weekend excursions to explore the public land heritage and provide a perspective that the agencies really need if they're going to transition successfully. We've gone in a relatively short period of time from a footprint that was substantially rural and substantially urban/suburban to one that is just decidedly urban/suburban, and that trend hasn't ended. We're going to top out at about 80 percent urban based on the latest projections. So finding ways to connect people back to the lands and waters that sustain is good and worthy work, and I'm really privileged to be able to do it. I take hundreds of kids with me and off we go . . .

Altogether this month we'll have a couple hundred students out, and each and every one of those students makes a choice to take time away from work, take time away from study to be about bigger things. If our generation, which does have a lot of access to resources, will use that access to remove the barriers for the next generation to experience these resources, I am now 100 percent convinced that the millennials will be there. It won't be about age; it won't be about gender; and it won't be about ethnoracial background. It will be about the strengths of this generation.

Another tells a story of how students who provide assistance to people outside the institution gain a strong sense of satisfaction from applying basic elements of their own knowledge and being of service to others in need:

Volunteer Income Tax Assistance is an IRS-sponsored program to help lower-income people have free tax preparation and get them earned income credits, education credits, and things like that. I teach a tax class in the fall, and I got five of my students to come and volunteer in the VITA program. It was the best thing I've ever done. First of all, you're teaching this conceptual stuff, and even though you give them tax software and have them prepare returns, this real-world experience is unbeatable. You get them sitting down with somebody who is divorced and trying to claim their kid, but then, "Wait a second, the father. The divorce decree says you can claim them, but the father is the custodial parent. He's got to sign this form, or otherwise, we can't claim them on your return." "Oh, he would never sign that." "The court decree says it and we used to be legally able to attach the court decree. No more." Anyway, you see this life experience of what these people go through. We'd have the site open until 9:00 p.m., and I've been there since 7:30 in the morning. It's going on fourteen and a half hours and they're excited. "What about this one? What about this one?" And we'd stay there until ten thirty at night talking about these things. Those students get so excited, and they come back. Now I've got almost twenty volunteers, and now I don't have enough clients for them. Talk about real-life experiences.

Faculty members teaching in programs that prepare students for certification in a service profession understand well the importance of experiential learning to prepare their graduates to function well in their chosen careers—and to be competitive in the market for entry-level jobs:

My premise is that the health and wellness exercise industry is so competitive that I don't want anyone to graduate with just a degree. There are about thirty professional organizations in the health and wellness industry, but only four of them have both content exams as well as practical exams. So you can get certified, but you need to do a workshop to do this. An example I use with students is, "My golden retriever is certified by eighteen different professional organizations as a certified personal trainer, and he has a great personality, and he loves to run. But that is not the kind of certification that you want to have." That resonates with my students. I tell them that as freshmen and they still as juniors are saying, "How can I get certified the right way?" They understand that it's not just a degree, but it also teaches them how to go out and market themselves and interview, talk about what their preparation is, et cetera, et cetera. That certification allows our students to understand the world that they're going into. It allows them to gain meaning for what it is that they're going to experience.

Even given all this extra benefit, certification is not a graduation requirement here, because developmentally, some kids just don't figure it out that soon. I mean, they're just behind. And our students are absolutely authentic; they want to be educated, but they come from all different backgrounds. Some of them start way the heck back, and it takes them a while to figure it out. I don't think that we're any less responsible for those kids than we are for the kids that start right away. We try to provide these opportunities for everyone, but I have students a year or two out and they'll call and say, "All right, I get it, I get it. When is the workshop? When do I have to do this?"

Here's the one that I love to drop, OK. If you go to a particular Ivy League university and you go to the athletic department, and you look at their strength and conditioning program, and you look at the coaches that are running the strength and conditioning program, you will find that they are all our grads. Can you believe it? I mean, it's unbelievable what our kids are doing.

However strong the affirmation of experiential learning in professional fields preparing students for specific careers, experiential education can have a hard time gaining support in more traditional academic disciplines. Sometimes the faculty member's role as an agent of such learning includes a certain amount of professional and even personal risk. In the most basic sense, students enter a learning environment in which the class leader has very little direct control. The professor may or may not accompany students in their assignments, and the relationship to students can evolve beyond teacher or mentor to that of coach or counselor. The students' learning may well exceed the domain of a faculty member's expertise—and as such, the professor whose course includes out-of-class components may be subject to criticism by traditional voices who assert that experiential education has no place in the academy because we have no criteria to evaluate it.

One of the most compelling narratives we heard in this vein came from a faculty member at an institution seeking to advance in the realm of higher education rankings. The general strategy was to develop programs stressing both distinctiveness and academic strength. For a set of reasons, including student responses to the choice of two curricular pathways as well as personal factors, this faculty member chose to replace a major writing assignment with a project that instead allowed students to work directly in service roles with members of a local community. (See in this volume "Faculty Voice: An Experiment in Experiential Learning" following chapter 2.)

PUTTING IT ALL TOGETHER

The stories told and insights recounted in this chapter derive, for the most part, from faculty members in their individual capacities. Implied in all these accounts, however, is a broader institutional context in which all faculty would confirm that theirs is but one of many influences on their students' learning. In fact, it is the totality of a student's learning experience that shapes the choices made and actions taken throughout life. While some stories here have derived from teachers of specialized programs, the more pervasive context is the broad liberal arts curriculum, and most faculty speak as one member of an academic community that offers education in a range of disciplines. Some recount their interest in witnessing the effect of this educational journey from a student's first enrollment to graduation:

I had a student who came in first day and said what 70 percent at least of our students say: "I want to be premed; I want to be a doctor or at least to do something in the health sciences." And I said to this student, "OK, why don't you take some chemistry, maybe a little math, and then what else do you like? Let's look at some other things." And she grabbed onto the liberal arts, and she took a theater course, acting; she took a dance course; and she loved art so she took a painting course. And she took the sciences and did well. She was very smart. This person who wanted to be a doctor just loved the liberal arts, and she just embraced that. It was so fun to work with her. She ended up, and I kind of laugh when I say this, of all the things she could have majored in, she decided to major in English in the end. I always laugh, but there's so much you can do with an English major.

The ultimate question that faculty members consider is how their own fields of study, their own academic disciplines and teaching methods become part of their students' larger learning experience in the curriculum and part of a student's identity and vocation in life. One of the most apt and compelling expressions of the relationship of individual faculty to one another, to the curriculum as a whole, and to the identity of the institution came in this observation from a professor in the performing arts:

> This institution is hundreds of years old. For many students who are here right now on this campus, this institution is a moniker or a part of the legacy of their families. So if we start to open this place up to different ways or thoughts or people or cultures, then it's going to take another at least four generations to make it a part of the institutional fabric, to make it real for everyone who's participating.
>
> We're starting by asking ourselves and our students to think through questions about themselves. Where are they situating themselves not only in the discipline of dance, but where is dance situating itself in their life? What do they know about the language or the discipline of dance that is akin to everything else we want to create as a liberal arts experience? And if I can figure that out, then I think we move closer toward the kind of synthesis about how a faculty is actually creating an institutional identity. I think if every program sat down and tried to situate itself within the realm of a liberal arts experience rather than taught its discipline inside a liberal arts structure, the curriculum would change by leaps and bounds. I think. That's just me. I go back to one of my colleagues who is a wonderful education studies professor and talks a lot about the liberal arts as making sense of the human experience. That's interesting to me as a dance

professor, because we also talk about art as a reflection of the human experience. If we understand that what we're doing in the liberal arts is pulling together a synthesis of ideas that ultimately creates a human life inside and outside of the institution, then learning, which I think is the art, is the reflection of that synthesis. I think there are a lot of tangible bridges to be made across disciplines.

Through any number of means and contexts, faculty are bridges—agents of passage and transport, helping students overcome impediments to progress and pursue roads to opportunities that may have first appeared as distant, unattainable prospects. In 1895, the British novelist Thomas Hardy published *Jude the Obscure*, which begins with its protagonist gazing from afar at the spires of Christminster University (a fictional equivalent of Oxford). Those towers of the academy symbolize his determination to advance in life through education, though Jude never succeeds in entering the university because of his social class. The faculty of U.S. institutions readily subscribe to the vision of empowering students of any background to achieve their goals through education. They offer pathways that help students connect with their aspirations, avert the sloughs of despond, and attain the goals that might have seemed distant and even foreboding.

The larger challenge that faculty face, however—and the subject of this book—is how they work collectively to create programs of learning that bring together different disciplines, teaching skills, educational philosophies, and methods as a coherent whole that provides students what they need to succeed in the twenty-first century.

Faculty Voice

TAKING OWNERSHIP

This storyteller taught advanced journalism students before becoming one of the pioneer instructors in a newly conceived general education program at a comprehensive university. Her own contribution to that program is a course that focuses on community engagement.

I teach a writing-intensive interdisciplinary class called "Telling Stories for Fun, Profit, and World Peace." Yeah, I made up that title so that it would allow me to tell investigative stories of all sorts. Because I only had really advanced journalism students and this was a class with no journalism students, it was really weird, and I didn't know how to scale back this type of class. I have nursing, business, communication, kinesiology, environmental studies students. I mean, nobody is from a field that I'm very familiar with. The idea was that I wanted my students to walk away with a deeper appreciation of storytelling, but I had to convince them that despite the discipline they belong in and/or will enter, they will need to understand this power of storytelling. Who is telling the story of the Ebola crisis, or health care reform, or the Wall Street crises? We are storytellers as humans, and our stories connect us as humans. They shape our world, and they shape the way we behave. So that's the class I'm teaching right now, and it is really fun.

I always have this giant project at the end of the semester for my students, and in past projects, we published an eighty-page, full-color book. They do podcasting with journal entries and things like that, and I put it up online so it's there for the masses. I believe that you take greater ownership when you know many eyes are on something, not just the eyes of your one professor.

For my general education class, my students are responsible for maintaining this brand-new site, which was inspired by "Humans of New York." That storytelling blog has spawned many, many other "Humans," but what I've noticed with others is they probably go into it thinking, "This is going to be great; I get to tell stories of my neighborhood or whatever," but then they realize that it's a lot of work to go out and to talk to people, get them to show a little bit of themselves, take a picture, come back, write it up, and post it. The guy in New York has found a way to sustain himself. Then I thought, "Well, heck, this would be a great way for the students in this class to see a world outside of their circle of ten friends, and a blog like this also allows me to sustain this model because every semester I'll have twenty-five more students going out and being the 'Humans' storytellers." We just started this semester, and in three weeks, we already have almost 1,800 followers! We've already posted about fifty stories.

Am I a contributor? I do about one out of ten stories, because I still want to show them what I'm talking about. Also, I want to keep my hand in it too. It's scary for them, but it's really fun for me. I set parameters, because if I tell them to produce ten "Humans" stories, they would just interview their friends. They have to interview somebody who's under the age of ten with the parent's permission; somebody over the age of seventy; a person of color because we do have people of color here; a person who works behind a counter, any counter; a person with disabilities; a laborer; an executive. I think they have two "freebies" out of those ten, because I want them to see that even though on the surface this is not that diverse racially, we are incredibly diverse.

In past projects with my graduate students, we produced these books about our student veterans, so I've had a relationship with the veterans in our community. Since this course is already a completely new thing for me, I didn't want to start something completely new, so I decided to add to the blog something with the veterans. Each semester from now on will focus on the overall "Humans" and then a subset of the humans, and this semester it's veterans.

The students work in small groups and have, I think, nine veterans and do more in-depth stories on them. At the end of the semester, we're actually going to produce a 150-page book with all the stories together, the "Humans" stories together with the veterans' stories. It will also have short reflections from each student on each encounter. What was their takeaway from the short interaction? Those reflections will not have appeared on the site itself, but they will be in the book as something extra and something cool, their reflections on how they've come to understand what they've learned. It's not just for a grade.

This is just some of what my students write every week. I haven't edited them, so there are typos in there. I just grabbed those and just copied and pasted them. Look at the third one; the third one is very interesting because she was very shy, but I made her go up and interview people. I made them all feel a little discomfited, you know? I was just superpleased with these reactions. One student and I were butting heads on one of her stories and her approach. She was very uncomfortable approaching people, but then she went to a public arena downtown and just sat in the park area and started looking at people to see if she could find someone who seemed approachable without feeling like she was being a stalker or a creep or something like that. And she saw a man who kind of reminded her of her dad. She went up to him and introduced herself and said, "I'm a student, and we're doing a project." She explained to him what she was doing, showed him the documentation for the project, and asked if he would mind talking with her for a little bit. He said, "Of all days, today," and she just waited, and he said, "I just had to put my dog down." And she said, "Oh, I'm so sorry."

They then spent two hours chatting. By the end, he was carrying a camera. He was taking pictures and told her he's going to start his own production company and said, "You should help me with this or work for me after graduation," so they exchanged information. I mean, she made a connection with a man who really needed to talk. Well, she didn't put that in her reflections. As I was reading the reflections, I said, "Oh, my gosh, how come you didn't put that in your reflections?" She said, "That's not for public consumption. He was just telling me that story." I tried to convince her that it's a better story if she puts that little part in there, but she wouldn't. She would not. I mean she just wouldn't. I first thought she was being really cocky, but when I went home, I kept thinking about this and thinking about this. My background is in journalism, so my ideal story is for the masses, and you want to get human emotion and everything in the story. But I wrote her a note the next day which said, "After giving some more thought, I want to tell you that you taught me a lesson yesterday. Not all stories are made for the masses. Some we only tell ourselves or maybe to a kind stranger who stopped to listen. I'm glad you stood your ground."

I am so pleased with the stories that these students are coming up with. Creating a culture of conversation in our community is exactly what I was hoping would happen.

CHAPTER 2

Why We Do What We Do

THE SPARK THAT IGNITES a faculty career comes early for some, later for others. Often the tale begins with a sense of intellectual purpose that becomes a steady drive beyond the baccalaureate. After this initial college degree comes graduate study, which, if that is successful and one is lucky, leads to a tenure-track appointment as an assistant professor. For others, the journey is not so straightforward and includes forays into different careers and identities. Regardless of season of life or vocational wanderings, when the spark occurs, its impact is unmistakable. One of the most poignant expressions of the power of learning as an agent of both intellectual and vocational transformation we heard came from a computer science professor, who told of his own trajectory through education:

> I'm fascinated by higher education. I'm definitely the first in my family to go to college. My mom was a bookkeeper, and we were poor. She never pushed me to go to school. I dropped out of high school in tenth grade, and I learned a trade. I learned how to build chain link fences, and then I bought my own truck and tools, became a licensed contractor, and then started a fence company. At about twenty-four or twenty-five years old, I realized I didn't want to dig holes in the Las Vegas heat all my life, so I decided to go to college, and I'm still not done. I just got my proposal approved for a dissertation. I'm in a doctoral program, and I'm sixty years old. Well, that's been dragging on way too long, because I do all these other things and lose focus sometimes. I feel what higher education has done for me should be shared. I see more and more of education pushed toward privatization, which I think is just sad, because there are some people like me who, without grants and loans and student aid, would have never been able to attend college. It's made my life just so much richer.

LIVES OF GROWTH THROUGH LEARNING

No one should doubt just how much colleges and universities have changed over the last sixty-plus years. From the Second World War forward, the image of the academy as a cloistered community has given way to one of openness and active engagement. Through all these changes, however, the primary bond linking faculty and institutions remains an unfettered commitment to professional independence. It is a perspective that faculty members are quick to volunteer as a testament to their identity and their work:

> We have a second-year course, which we developed through a grant from the National Endowment for the Arts. It's sitting around a table talking about beautiful books and ideas, and I think that space should always be cherished and fought for here. Particularly in the United States, which has sort of an anti-intellectual culture, it is really, really important to preserve these intellectual spaces because they matter.

The opportunity to continue learning as both a scholar and a citizen was an animating principle repeatedly voiced by faculty members reflecting on their careers. Very often these statements conjoin with statements of the satisfaction that comes from teaching students. The freedom to organize a learning process—for one's students, or for one's self, in ways of one's own choosing—is a powerful motivator. For a mathematics professor, it was the excitement of learning that resulted from establishing different relationships among his students and between him and them that makes for a truly two-way learning process:

> The reason that I like winter term is partly selfish. I see it as a vehicle for experimenting with things and doing new things and moving into new areas, where in our department in a curriculum as structured as mathematics curricula, it's harder to do that. The last winter term course that I taught was in very computer-intensive methods for dealing with statistical questions and randomness, with lots and lots of simulation and resampling. I had only twelve students, and it was full. It was limited to twelve students because it was designed to meet a college writing requirement, which tends to make it a little bit more appealing to some students. And I just had a wonderful time with that course.
>
> For one thing, I felt like I was almost a student alongside my students. Now that doesn't mean that I don't have a lot more context and background. I certainly do, but there were some open-ended questions that we looked at together. I divided the students up into four teams of three. They worked on projects together. They reported out in class. And I really think it worked pretty well. It was really new for me and I think for them. I think of that as an almost unexpected success story, and all but one of my students presented something at the spring student research symposium that year.

And then, as is almost always the case in the academy, there were those whose stories focused on the other side of the coin, often observing in their colleagues a propensity to take excessive license with intellectual freedom, to the point of making change and contrariness values themselves. The most these faculty will concede is that change can be necessary, provided that it is an impulse tempered by a habit of leaving intact those things that seem to be working just fine, thank you:

> I'm not one who believes in change for change's sake. I believe in change because it makes things work better, but there is still an important way in which continuity is vital. There's always a complicated spectrum of things that should and shouldn't happen in terms of change. It is important to think about innovation and change where they are necessary and not be afraid of them. It is also important to have a certain continuity, especially when it comes to liberal arts, because you can't really have change without continuity; otherwise, it's meaningless. Those are principles to which I'm committed, and there is still at the core of the liberal arts mission, the ancient mission, the concept of making people good citizens of their city-state as it were.

Here is the same idea expressed differently:

> I think what I have seen here is that a group of faculty will get excited about a particular idea and will go chase that particular idea. They get the structure set up . . . and then they go chase a different idea. So we have these orphaned programs. It's a case of "Oh, here's a new shiny object to go play with now!"

A faculty career means being surrounded by colleagues with a shared set of academic values including a common commitment to continued growth and learning. Many attest to the richness of conversations in the lunch room or the hallways. Sometimes these dialogues advance to the extent that individual faculty members venture into collaboration, yielding teaching projects that benefit students while also enriching the intellectual lives of the faculty themselves. In many cases, however, the tales of working together with a colleague conclude with a sense of exasperation at the organizational constraints that lay waste to so many good opportunities.

There is, at the same time, a clear sense of how a really good college education ought to foster interdependence among different academic skills and departments, as noted by this professor of nursing:

> One of the major complaints that we have as nurses is that nurse students should be able to write. I know society has changed and everyone's gone

to texting, and even in the hospital, some people are texting physicians, but communication will always remain the same. You've got to be able to communicate, and we're asking students to do research, and they don't know how to write a research paper, or they don't know how to deliver a speech. We get these papers, and I'm like, "Oh, my gosh, this is something you'd see in third grade." I'm not an English major, but I know where to put a comma, and I know how to build an argument. In nursing, you have to communicate constantly. My students aren't going out and writing big, long nurses' notes, but as they go on, I fear their inability to write is going to be an issue for them in their master's or doctoral programs.

Some of our faculty conversations included a call for an institutional structure that values interdisciplinary approaches to accomplish educational purposes. The underlying complaint, to be sure, is not just with the home institution but with the fact that academic disciplines hold tremendous power both within individual universities and colleges and across the span of higher education:

> The faculty here are very disciplinary based. I think people are afraid for their jobs. We have seen in geography that people who have been trained in interdisciplinarity cannot teach what we think is important, even as a basic course in geography. Training is important, and I must say that when I advise students to go to graduate school and they want to do Middle East studies or Central Asian studies, I tell them that they must have some discipline to go with it or they will not get a job. As long as schools hire in disciplines, the applicant with an interdisciplinary graduate degree won't be viewed the same as somebody who finished in a discipline.

Often lost in this clash of disciplinary values are the avocational interests of faculty interested in two or more, often quite disconnected, disciplines. What follows is a story from a liberal arts chemistry professor with a passion for Greek literature. His is a story that makes clear just how important a faculty member's ability to roam can be:

> Greek literature has always been a hobby of mine. I was teaching Homer, Aeschylus, and Aristophanes at my last institution. The expectation there was that everybody would teach at least one of their course units outside of their major, and I think that's great. No, I'm not a literature scholar, but I have opinions, and I have the ability to read. Students have opinions too, and they have the ability to read. Just because something is the written word, whether it's Homer or whether it's Descartes, doesn't mean that you have to have someone from that area lead a discussion that's going to help students develop an appreciation and make it relevant, whether

it was three thousand years ago or whether it was from three months ago. I mean, do you have to have that kind of a degree? I think we have a territorial bent that there has to be some kind of professional vetting on who can teach what, but as long as I'm not saying, "I'm going to teach this class in Greek literature and I want it to be a 300-level course in the English major," and instead I'm saying, "I'm going to teach this course on Homer and Aeschylus and I want to do it at the 100 level," why not? I want students to see how these ancient Greeks were so much like us: like our modern athletes or our modern politicians. I find that niche that connects with the student athletes, poli-sci majors. "If you're a chemist, look at what they're doing here engineering-wise. Look at what they're doing in terms of their planning and how they're changing things. Think about the mysticism that's present in what they're doing." We can find those things, and we can talk about them. Just because I'm not an English scholar shouldn't disqualify me from being able to lead a seminar about Greek literature. This is one of the things that I believe very strongly in.

DIFFERING VIEWS

Notwithstanding the academy's celebration of collegiality, no one should be surprised that there are matters on which faculty members disagree, at times vehemently. A concentration of independent thinkers naturally gives rise to differences on matters both large and small within an institution, including different views of the purpose and goals of education. For a professor of social work, the principle animating her career was the ability to be engaged as well as thoughtful:

> I love what I do. You know, there are social justice issues that take place on campus and that need to be addressed, and then there are social justice issues that occur off campus, and they need to be addressed. So for me, that is a common thread in terms of all the work that I do, whether I make a decision about admissions or I make a decision about a policy or I make a decision about how I teach, that thread works its way through.

A professor of dance similarly supported the incorporation of active learning approaches that engage students with environments beyond the classroom setting as a means to both experience issues in societal contexts and explore one's own identity:

> So what we've tried to do in thinking about the role of embodied scholarship is make more space on campus and in the curriculum for students to be able to activate their learning, whether that be through movement or

writing or some other type of creative modality, but also give them the opportunity to share the way that their learning is shaping their perception of the world and their identity. And I think that is the curricular shift we're watching actually happen, the shift away from didactic learning and rhetoric to actual action and thought processes that are relevant to students today as they come in so that they don't have to check their identities at the classroom doors and then become a rote learner.

Others worry, though, about the forces they perceive as drawing their institutions away from learning modes that emphasize study and reflection and toward avenues of direct action and engagement. We encountered stories reflecting the consternation of faculty who saw faddish changes as a retreat from the notion that the academy ought to encourage the cultivation of thought and understanding as an end in itself:

> There's huge support for sustainability across the faculty, so that wasn't such a controversy for most people in our discussions about the new core. They saw it as an extension of what they were doing anyway. I don't see it quite as strongly as representing a liberal arts core. Although I'm happy that students are getting lots of impetus to study sustainability and to think about the environment, it's less central from a liberal arts perspective. The aim of education is knowledge, and while knowledge should lead to action, we don't want to give the impression that a course is only social action or we cease to be an educational institution.
>
> I just finished thirty-three reviews for the Fulbright scholarship program, and some applications became very focused on social activism. I think institutions and scholarship generally have to guard a little bit against trends toward becoming socially active institutions and not primarily educational institutions. I just want to make sure constantly that the inquiry, the improvement of knowledge, the improvement of intellectual qualities is balanced. Education should be the cause of social action rather than the social action being dominant. I think that's the difference between being an educational institution and being a think tank lobbying the government.

Then there was the divide between those of their colleagues who affirm a classic liberal arts mission—to educate students in the realms of knowledge and impart skills of critical thinking and expression—and those who conceive education as drawing students into relation with practical and applied issues in society. Here a historian at a liberal arts college delineates the divide:

> It may be different at big universities or community colleges, but the issue at a liberal arts college is that there's a crisis of identity and a struggle

with delivering an education that's relevant, whatever that means. That's heightened by the increased cost of education.

There are a number of different responses to this crisis. There are some who decide they need to have a very narrow focus and look very intently at the work they do—whether they are classicists or biologists or historians as I am—to say that there is value in their particular field. Critics of that would say that they are blind to the broader world and that they're simply just digging down on their own arcane literature and finding value in that. Then there's a whole group of other faculty who are eager to make their learning applied, as they call it, and as a result are trying to go outside of the four walls of the classroom and to engage communities in town or in other ways to make the learning of the students more similar to a preprofessional program. There's seemingly some tension between that and the other group.

I think the challenge that liberal arts colleges have is to find a structure, a curriculum that's going to accommodate both perspectives and other perspectives as well. The changes that will take place in a liberal arts curriculum over the next ten, fifteen, twenty years are going to be changes that recognize that the traditional value of in-classroom experience— the trench work of teaching a student to say, "My name is Ingrid" in Spanish—is equally as valuable as experiential learning where a faculty member says, "I'm going to take my students to the local soup kitchen, and we're going to learn about the economics of poverty by interacting with those who take advantage of this service." Those are two very different approaches to education, and they have two different philosophies in some regard. They're both equally valid, but the challenge of liberal education now is going to be how we create the structure whereby students are able to take advantage of both without feeling that they're walking from one end of campus to another end of campus.

STRUCTURES THAT CONSTRAIN

Apart from philosophical differences about educational purposes and modes, the college and university faculty whose stories we collected worried that organizational and governance structures too often distorted the character of teaching and learning at their institutions. Particularly in universities and colleges with a strong foundation in the liberal arts, faculty members saw a diminution of learning as a process of broad inquiry and the trying out of different fields of study. Too often this ideal devolves to a program in which the demands of the major effectively usurp students' ability to explore widely beyond the straits of focused study in their primary field. While the course roster presents itself as a generous expanse of opportunities students might explore, some faculty observe that the embedded constraints reduce the full possibilities for extended learning.

Many pointed out that one of the primary obstacles blocking curricula that promote broad learning is the students themselves. The cost of higher education is an incentive to ensure that the course of study has a practical outcome in a job or career. A natural instinct of students, which is a source of distress to many faculty members, is to focus on the major to the extent of constraining the exploration of other topics—and to focus on grades, often at the expense of learning to the full extent of their capabilities. As often as not, that sense of exasperation was worn for all to see:

> My personal hobbyhorse right now is that I'm convinced that the number one problem educationally here and at many schools like this is liberal grading within our culture. It's something that students bring with them, and the question is, Are they motivated by grades or are they motivated by learning?
>
> I have a fifteen-year-old daughter who's a sophomore in high school right now, and she's a really smart, great student. She says—and I don't think she's saying it just to please me—that she doesn't care what grade she gets. Last semester she got all A-pluses, except for in her English class, where she got an A. She was most happy with that A because she worked harder for that A than for any of the A-pluses, and she felt like she learned more in getting that. It showed her that her teacher had some standards and did not simply give out an A-plus to the smartest kid in the class.
>
> My daughter isn't motivated by grades. She's motivated by learning, but for the system in which she's working and the colleges to which she will be applying, grades are the measurable outcome that you can point to. Once students come to college, there's very or comparatively little point to grading for the next step. There are few places where it matters, so I really want to see a school like this radically rethink what grades are and how they operate. I think they currently serve as an impediment to learning rather than a motivation or accountability mechanism to learning. That's my reform passion right now.

A further abridgment of interest in curricular explorations occurs as a result of students pursuing double majors, thereby increasing the number of requirements to be met through enrollments in two different programs. Students often regard this practice as a way of increasing their marketability after graduation; at the same time, it may add years to their degree completion. A faculty member in mathematics at a liberal arts college explains the impact of double majors on course taking in the liberal arts:

I do think that the liberal arts are pretty important, because they provide wonderful opportunities to explore as undergraduates at a four-year liberal arts college. They won't have the time and the opportunities to explore things and learn things later in life when they have to work to earn a living and support a family and on and on and on, at least not until they retire. Maybe when they retire, I think, right?

I happen to love music, and when I was an undergraduate, I loved philosophy, even though my areas were mathematics and physics. But I really do value those kinds of things. My department a couple of years ago voted out the structure of dual degrees, and the consequence of that is that we have more and more double majors among our students. The most common double majors are mathematics and economics; mathematics and computer science; mathematics and physics; sometimes mathematics and neuroscience and mathematics and environmental studies. We do get math and music once in a while, and we've had students actually do senior theses that cross both disciplines. I love it when that happens.

But if you want to talk about something that stands in the way of the liberal education that I value, it's all the students who choose two majors, one in mathematics and one in economics, or one in mathematics and one in computer science. There's a barrier to liberal education. In my advising, I strongly urge students to consider one major and then to take all the courses that they want to and like in another area, to not constrain themselves by having to take every last course to meet the technical requirement of a double major. Nobody's going to care when they look at a transcript after graduation. I'm absolutely sure that's right. But it's hard to convince students of that. Partly, it's not so much the students sometimes as it is the parents behind the scenes. I see this, particularly with our international students.

As a result of these constraints, there is a sense among many faculty members that they inhabit a landscape that limits their ability to develop curricula that explore and expand their own as well as their students' horizons. Often, the ideal of learning as embodied in the liberal arts education—to explore broadly and learn from a range of knowledge—gets distilled into structures and customs that emphasize focused achievement over breadth of knowledge. In the academy itself, the liberal arts have been increasingly subject to disaggregating forces that, by subdividing knowledge into succinct units, exert increasing power over the curriculum and student enrollment:

> We need to learn together how to do interdisciplinary education, and in some ways, I think the humanities are more naturally able to be interdisciplinary. If you were to ask me what I teach, I can't distinguish what

I do from history from literature or from philosophy or religion. I cross over those boundaries every day in class. I can't teach what I teach without teaching history. I can't teach what I teach without raising philosophic questions. The traditional liberal arts disciplines tend to be humanities rooted and humanities based. And from there they branch out. I'm not at all unhappy about having a math requirement or a science requirement, but I think the centrality of the humanities in the whole curriculum isn't always understood. Let me use philosophy as an example, because I teach philosophy classes. There's a tendency to see a philosophy course as one course that you plug in for a requirement amongst many. Yeah, you've fulfilled that. But that's not exactly the way a true philosophic inquiry would work because what gets done in philosophy is more ubiquitous. It's across the board. It's more a kind of governing science. In the departmentalization that we have in the institution, and all institutions, it is one more department among many, which puts philosophy—puts the humanities generally, I think—in a bit of an awkward position.

Reluctant Leaders

We began this chapter with the observation that people come to a faculty career at different seasons in life, and in many cases their entry into this profession follows time spent doing other jobs. The reflections of those who have come to the academy from other occupations often testify why so many outside the academy find what faculty do to be peculiar. A professor of management explained,

> I've studied management for a long time. I grew up in the Air Force, where they teach you leadership and all this stuff. It's such a different philosophy and mode of operating at this organization or probably at any college. Even as a chair, I can't say, "You're fired." You just can't do that kind of thing, which is probably good. It's not that you want to do that, but it is also difficult to understand. "Am I your boss or am I not your boss?" This would never be the case in the corporate world, but we work as a profession with collegiality. You just hope you all get along, but that doesn't happen.
>
> The other thing I've noticed is that a lot of faculty never had the experience of managing people. I did in the Air Force, because I had jobs, so I understand it. But I see other faculty across the university, where there may be a philosophy professor or an English professor saying, "Did you ever work in the world outside of college?" I mean, you just have to understand what motivates people and how to treat them, and I think this is hard for some people because they may never have had that experience.

Just as telling as an expression of the uniqueness of a faculty environment is the account of a former police officer who now serves as chair of a
criminal justice department. It was his experience leading a precinct—and not
his schooling as an academic—that equipped him for becoming an academic
administrator:

> I went back to school about ten years ago in anticipation that there would
> be a life after law enforcement. My second career has always been edu-
> cation and teaching. I taught for several institutions in the region, until
> I focused and settled here as a kind of postretirement job until my six-
> ties, and I'll bet I'll do at least another ten years. I like what I do; I love
> what I do.
>
> Teaching is the same thing as when I was with the police department.
> I was a problem solver. I fix things. I retired as a commander, but in our
> rank structure, a commander runs a bureau, like a precinct. In my last
> command, I had two precincts. My whole career was being sent places to
> problem solve, to fix things.
>
> Whenever I came into a precinct, our assignments were three-year
> assignments. In a typical precinct, you've got usually about somewhere
> between eight and ten issues. OK, process map it out; which ones are
> most critical, and attack three of those. You have one on deck, one in
> the hole, and you just keep that motion in a proven problem-solving
> model. One of these models that I like best, called Scanning, Analysis,
> Response, and Evaluation (SARA), has an absolutely universal fit in any
> profession.
>
> The problem with past models is that bosses usually come in, assess,
> and then drive the solution down. Well, what SARA does is the reverse of
> that. You truly seek input from the lowest level, so in education, you'd go
> to faculty. The next level you'd go to would be the chairs. The next level
> you go to would be the deans. Then you look at your stakeholders—your
> user groups—and if there's any other group that wants to be heard, you
> listen to them. And then you process map everything they say. You listen
> to them and say, "What are your top three? You've given me twenty items,
> and I can't fix twenty items. What are your top three?" And you then try
> to find some synergy, some way of pulling those together. The analysis is
> just, "OK, let's look at dollars and cents. Let's look at what resources I can
> bring to bear on this, if any. Where are my land mines going to be? What
> are my user groups that are going to be the most vocal?" And that analysis
> happens before you start your plan, and then you just attack it.

Many of those faculty leaders and managers who did not come to higher
education from another career found the transition to academic leadership

more difficult. In fact, comparatively few of those who begin a faculty career following graduate study envision administrative leadership as a professional goal. A first foot in the water for many is to chair a department—a task for which few have received any previous training. More than previous experience, the inherent criterion for leadership in the academy is that one be a member of the faculty. At the department level, it is regarded as a service role, sometimes described as a period in which one "stands" as chair and attends to administrative details for two or three years and then steps down, resuming a role as faculty member among colleagues. The basic skills of leadership in the academy do not differ greatly from those of other professions—the ability to listen, to hear different sides of disputes, to negotiate differences, to reconcile academic goals with financial resources. The key difference is the fact that, beyond a certain point, an academic leader does not have much authority over those he or she leads.

What nonetheless motivates faculty members to assume greater administrative responsibilities is often a commitment to the same values that initially moved them to seek a faculty career—to sustain what is valuable and to change what has become ineffective. Often the trigger that propels a step into leadership is the realization that institutional factors that have provided the context for quality teaching and learning are undergoing change and that the outcome could go well or badly, depending on who is in charge. A story told by a faculty member who chairs a first-year experience program at a regional public university nicely sums up the why of administration service:

> I had made up my mind that I was going to just think of my teaching as a job, stop thinking of it in terms of a career. I was going to wear a lot of jeans and have an office with my favorite fellow faculty member with a couch and a fridge. I'd sail into my last twenty years or something in that fashion. When I made that decision that year and really gave up, this position opened up for a director of the first-year experience program.
>
> At that point I was probably teaching three classes and was also overseeing the writing support program, which had classes of ten students, each overseen by a trained student. These students worked on their writing for their regular writing class. I sat in on a bunch of these classes to try to understand my new role in the new world I was in, and these students could not understand what the hell was going on at the university. They were saying, "Yeah, in my history class, they're making me listen to these lectures, and I just took history in high school" or "Yeah, in my science class, they're making me chew crackers and spit them out, and I don't know why" or "In my English class, they won't let me say anything I think. I have to find out what other people think." And I thought, "Oh,

my god, we're doing a terrible job, a terrible job. These students don't know what a university is, and they, therefore, don't know what it affords them." Many of the students in these pull-out classes were minority students, and it became clear to me they were first generation. So when that first-year experience job opened up, even though it was a crazy huge job for me to spend only half of my overall time on, I applied for it because I thought, "We have to do better than this." My story at that point—just over ten years ago—took kind of an unusual turn.

Those who speak highly of their service as academic managers and leaders nearly always stress the learning they have gained from such service—including the discovery of skills one might never have had occasion to develop and apply—as attested to by a professor of mathematics at a community college who chairs his division:

> I love being division chair. I get a tremendous amount of satisfaction from that. I enjoy very much having challenges and problems to solve. A lot of my satisfaction in my work comes from problem solving, and so I found that as much as I enjoy teaching in the classroom, I wasn't using my entire skill set. As I was able to take on this chair role, it allowed me to continue to do some work in the classroom but also to work with college-level planning and dealing with operational and people issues. That complexity of the work I find very satisfying and fulfilling. A second thing that has been very rewarding for me, which is also about a five-year experience, was being on what we call our meet-and-confer team, which is our contract negotiation team. In that experience, I was negotiating with the administration and working alongside in a collaborative way with college presidents, vice chancellors, and other faculty. There were eight-person teams and negotiating solutions to those problems that faced the institution. I learned about politics and how you work things politically in an organization but also how to persuade people and work collaboratively with folks with diverse viewpoints, so a very enriching experience.

One of the most remarkable stories of leading a change process in an academic institution was told by a scholar who had enjoyed a satisfying career of nearly three decades as a research scientist in a large university. The step into an administrative position was not one that he had prepared for or sought until a moment arrived that made clear that change was coming and that deliberate attention would be required if the transition was to be successful.

As in other cases, his decision was motivated in part from a desire to help ensure the continued high caliber of the programs involved and to help make sure the process maintained a sense of collegiality among those most directly affected. It is a story of acquiring different skills from those he had perfected in his faculty role. He learned the imperative of involving the faculty in every decision to be made and that the time required to achieve a transition within a school was twice as long as he had estimated. As it turns out, one of the most gratifying measures of his achievement was that a faculty member who had initially been a highly vocal critic ultimately reconsidered and became a leading proponent of the initiative after realizing that the proposed course of action was the best achievable for future faculty and students.

Finally, the story reaches a very satisfying conclusion—that is, the moment when he could "stand down" and resume a career as one who educates students and conducts research once again as a member of the faculty. Before leaving the deanship, he had worried whether a successor would come in with a different philosophy and undo everything he had achieved. He was fortunate to have found a colleague to inherit and carry forward his work:

> Eventually I was able to convince him. I have to take him out and buy him a beer every other week, but other than that, it works out pretty well. You know, it gives us both a chance—for me, to reminisce, and for him, to kind of let off steam. (See the long story "Faculty Voice: Stepping into the Fray" following chapter 7.)

The Return—What Keeps Us Here

Our chapter ends as it began, with the affirmation that, whatever its frustrations and constraints, professorial life in the academy comes nearer to personal and intellectual fulfillment than most other careers provide. Nothing else so fully embodies the learning and growth one had experienced as a student than the life of a faculty member whose journey continues with the engagement of new thinking and ideas in conjunction both with students and with faculty colleagues of one's own institution and beyond. It is a profession ripe with opportunities to expand one's own understanding by drawing on others' fields of expertise or from the inspiration of students who bring new visions of what can be achieved by working within or across the boundaries of established disciplines.

Because a college or university defines itself as a setting that affirms the latitude to explore and express ideas as fundamental, it follows that differing views arise on matters of substance as well as on the goals of teaching. These perspectives can be seen in part through the curriculum, as debates between traditional instruction and experiential learning or disagreements about the degree to which education should be infused with such goals as instilling a commitment to social activism. The differences can also appear as frustration about the structure and operations of institutions. There are expressions of dismay about rules that discourage collaboration and effectively impede students from gaining the extended benefits of sampling widely across the curriculum and realizing the potential for knowledge creation that stems from working across the boundaries of knowledge as represented in departments and disciplines.

Some of the most telling instances of new learning are from those who care so greatly about the vitality of their institution, school, or department that they become academic managers and leaders to help ensure that in periods of change, the most valuable elements of their educational programs can be sustained. Virtually everyone who takes this step into administration describes it as a major experience of learning and a defining moment in a career. Those who come into higher education from other professions express how very different the organization of the academy is from virtually any other kind of institution. Beyond the unique structure of authority and decision-making that derives from shared academic governance, the nature of leadership in higher education allows a faculty member to complete a season of service and return to a pure faculty role.

Returning to the faculty is an act of coming full circle—one that allows a person to take up habitation again in a realm of one's own choosing and definition. Those who return following a term of service as department chair, dean, or provost resemble, in many respects, those who had careers in other professions before entering the academy and gaining a faculty position. Very likely they regard the academic community of which they are a part with different eyes, having experienced directly the interactions, disputes, and financial anxieties that characterize decision-making in the academy.

Whether as an administrator or as a participant in a faculty governance process, the ultimate sanctuary for many occurs from reclaiming the realm of four walls in one's own classroom. It is in that setting, possibly more than any other, where the ability to create and advance one's own vision is least constrained. Whatever difficulty a university or college faculty may have in changing the curriculum of an institution, in the classroom itself, virtually any member of that faculty has substantial discretion in choosing—if not the absolute content—then certainly how to teach it. This is the space, more than any other, that causes faculty members to stay with their institutions despite their inevitable disappointments.

Faculty Voice

Hidden among the Artifacts

This storyteller is a tenured associate professor at a comprehensive university who had just been reelected by his colleagues for a third three-year term as director of the undergraduate program and is the past president of the faculty union. A social activist and community leader as well as an inveterate storyteller with an impressive command of his classroom, he approaches teaching in the same way that he works on behalf of his colleagues and neighbors. He believes the future social workers he teaches need to learn how to listen to the world around them and come to understand the sometimes harrowing stories their clients will tell. Drawing upon his own talents as a storyteller, he models how best to both tell a good story and how to listen purposefully to the tales other people tell.

I've got a young man who is going back to Africa, and he's a really interesting student. He is black, but he's not African American; he's black. His parents are both from Africa and unbeknownst to each other, they came to the United States to study. They met at college, fell in love, and got married. They had two sons. They had him and they had his older brother. I won't get into the story, but the parents ultimately divorced.

This young man was in my U.S. diversity class last semester. I said to him, "This is not the class where we're going to play 'Oh, my misery is worse than yours. Let me tell you the tale of the trail of tears. No, let me tell you about the internment camps in the United States. Well, let me tell you about being called a n—Well, no, let me tell you about being called a wetback, and, oh, let me tell you about when I was bullied in the bathroom.'" I said, "We're not going to do that. We're going to talk about what does privilege mean and what does it look like? And then we're going to talk about what do we do with this information. Why is this so important for people who are interested in working in human services? Because people are going to come in, in all sizes, shapes, colors, and political ideologies." And I said, "Most of them—not all, but most who come in to see social workers—are going to come from the bottom end of the socioeconomic status, and that's the straw that broke the camel's back."

This young man had never had a class like this. I had seventy under-graduate students in that class. The first assignment in the class, which takes half the semester to get through, is that everybody has to bring in an artifact. I tell them, "An artifact is something that represents a person, a family, a com-munity, a culture. I want you to bring in one artifact from your life, and you're going to tell us the story of you. You're going to tell us why you chose that artifact and why you are talking to us about this facet of your life. And I'll go first."

I tell them my story. I always bring in *molcajete*. Molcajete is M-O-L-C-A-J-E-T-E, a grinder in the kitchen. Molcajete is like a pestle and mortar in the Mexican culture. It's very rough and made of stone for grinding peppers and tomatoes and so forth. When you cook, you roast and then grind, or you grind when the ingredients are fresh. It's all different with all the types of foods that seep into it. And over the years molcajete acquires its own flavor, if you will.

I tell them that my family spent every weekend at my grandfather's house. I say, "Today I hear you guys talking about, 'Oh, this weekend is my kid's birth-day, and we're going to go to X place or we're going to have this theme and we had to send out all the invitations this week to invite all these kids.' Well, when I was a kid, it was just me and my cousins and my siblings, over sixteen of us, and that was just the kids. It was like an instant party every time we got together. My grandparents' house was the hub of the family. My grandfather was the patriarch, and he had this nice, big house with all these kids who were running around. It didn't matter that there was a front yard and patio and all these bedrooms, because everybody always congregated in the kitchen. The kitchen was the heart of that home. In that kitchen was where I learned about who I was and who my family was. How did we come to this country and why did we come to this country? Where did the journey start and how did it culminate in Los Angeles?"

I say to them, "I tell you that story because as you learn about this, you learn that family is very important for me. You learn that not only is family important, but celebrations to honor one another—whether it's a gradua-tion, a birthday, an anniversary—are important to our family. You can imagine that for an extended family, every weekend is a celebration for something. Somebody's got a birthday; somebody's got an anniversary; somebody's got a promotion. And it's also about food. You've got all these people crammed into a kitchen that's not even three-quarters the size of this room. They're all crammed in there, and everyone's laughing and talking. There'd be this uncle drinking too much and saying a little too much that he shouldn't say and maybe that kid over there is eating what's for dessert and we haven't even had dinner yet. Everyone's laughing. Do you get the picture?" And everyone in the class is laughing, and I'm wanting to be even more vivid about the smells and this and that. They're all passing around this molcajete.

Then every one of those seventy persons has the same experience. They tell stories about being biracial and being too dark for this side of the family and being too white for this side of the family. They tell stories about being homeless. I had one student who brought in a bag of Top Ramen, and I don't know if you know what Top Ramen is, but it's basically like instant noodles. She brought this ramen in, and she says, "This is my culture." And she goes into how both of her parents were drug addicts and really abdicated the responsibility of being parents. Her older sister who isn't that much older than she is wanted to make sure she ate every day, so she ate that ramen every single day growing up as a kid.

So they all tell their stories. Some people cry; they break down because they have horrible stories of discrimination, and this is why I keep this experience in my class. There's no writing. I tell everybody, "When your classmate is at the front of the class, everybody pays attention. No e-mails; don't check your text messages. I need you to be present. Because when you are working in human services, you need to be present for that person, when they're telling you these incredibly intimate details about their finance and their sex life and what goes through their brain first thing in the morning and last thing at night. You need to be present. You're going to start practicing that here."

How is it possible in a room of seventy people that a lot of times it only felt like there were two or three of us in the room? Because everything was so focused. All the attention was right there. The students were supportive of one another. Some people would break down, and people would come up—I didn't have to prompt them—and hug them and take them back to their seat. Then that would be it. Their story would be done, and they didn't need to elaborate anymore. For the young man whose parents were from Africa, he said, "You know, I think that I don't understand who I am or where I come from. I never had any interest in going to Africa before, but in that class, I realized, 'How can I go out as a social worker and help other people if I don't even know who I am?'" So he's going to be in Africa, and he's going to find out who he is.

I share this course with you because we're talking about curriculum. The thing that is important—for me, at least—is that you have to make connections for people because you can assign this book or that article or this movie or that whatever, but in the classroom, you've got to bring it together and people like stories.

Faculty Voice

AN EXPERIMENT IN EXPERIENTIAL LEARNING

After successfully surviving the tenure review process—writing, publishing, doing schol-arly research, teaching the old curriculum—this professor at a small college realized that she could finally teach her students in ways that would make an impact on their learning, their lives, and other people's lives at the same time. She shook up one of her favorite courses by eliminating an important composition assignment and used the time thus freed up to send her students into the community to experience, in real-world terms, what she was teaching them.

There's a tension between wanting *U.S. News & World Report* to put you in their top categories and focusing your attention on other things, but in that period of my life, I was an assistant professor, and it seemed like the focus of the college was a little bit more inward in a way. How do you show to others, how do you prove to others that you're good at what you do? That's the focus of a lot of assistant professors too because we have to get tenure.

Over the years some pretty sucky things have happened in my life. I mean incredibly book-worthy, *Dateline*-worthy, amazing, crazy, bad things. You get the idea. It has helped me sort of to shake out my feelings. What the hell. We only live once, and there is really important work to be learned and done. What do I want to do? As a result, I made some changes this cur-rent term that are really risky in a way. They're not risky for me person-ally because of my belief that you only live once, whatever, and because I have tenure—right—and honestly, this is for me the best representation that I've felt of my own feeling of tenure helping me.

I'm pushing the boundaries. I teach intercultural communication, and I am passionately committed to it, and there are amazing resources out there. Over the years, students have engaged, and they can write wonderful work, and I am proud of the class the whole time that I've taught it. However, I just took away a major paper assignment in order for my students to be able to devote hours to working with refugee families in the community. So in teams of three, my students partnered with World Relief, through which they have to spend ten to fifteen hours working on their own with refugee families in the community. They get trained, they've read about it, and they have a World Relief volunteer. Because all of the refugee families have to have background checks to get here, all of my students have to have background checks too. They are learning amazing things, and I'm proud of that.

At first, I might have felt like "How can I take away a major composition?" When you look on paper, my students are doing far fewer academic assignments. They have two three-page papers, and they have reading quizzes every day, but if I'm honest about what I want them to do and where I want them to spend their time, I want them to spend their time interacting. It's intercultural communication, and that's where a lot of the learning happens. So I took away that assignment. I look at my syllabus, and I think it sort of looks like—I'm going to maybe overstate it—I don't think it looks like a joke, but it doesn't look like, oh . . . an academically rigorous course. But I know, I know how rigorous it is.

It was hard for my students. I mean, they're shy. They're a little upset with me for demanding so much of their time outside the classroom. So there's a little pushback or there was a little pushback before they met their families. And now they're coming to class, and they're telling stories. I just had a phone call last night from a student who said, "Dr. S, I'm sorry I'm calling you at home, but we're with our family, and this family has been here two or three weeks from Ethiopia. And the mom. We were just making pizza because we had all these ideas of what can we do, trying to just spend time doing whatever they need. So we were just making pizza together, or the family is making pizza with us, and the mom wouldn't eat the pizza. She said, 'No, she couldn't.' And she showed us her scar from her C-section, and she went over to her side and said, 'You know next week.' And so, we think she's going to have surgery next week, but she thinks she can't eat anything until next week—only water. She said, 'Only water.'" They finally got from the mother that she was having surgery the next Wednesday. The students said to me, "Dr. S, we think she's not going to eat until next Wednesday, and we can't get her to eat."

Clearly there was a misunderstanding, but this stuff absolutely happens. Think of Mary Pipher, of *Reviving Ophelia* fame, who wrote a book called *The Middle of Everywhere*, which my students read. She volunteered with refugee families in Lincoln, Nebraska, and it's full of stories like that, so my students are coming to class telling stories exactly like we've been reading in this book.

Another group of students from this class found out that a school had turned away an eighteen-year-old refugee teenage girl because she wasn't going to be able to graduate on time. That's against the law. They were researching the law and calling me and asking me what I knew about the legal rights of refugees.

We're developing these plans working with World Relief and working with these families. They're doing, after one meeting, refugee advocacy, and in my heart of hearts, I know this is a class, this is a real class. Part of it came from my own personal belief in doing things while you can. Like I could be hit by a bus tomorrow. What do I want my students to learn? What do I need them to know about intercultural communication? We need to have them spend time doing these things.

I guess all this is to say my focus now has changed with what I see semi-reluctantly happening in overall curricula. I don't know if I can say it like that, but I don't think we should try to be a school that only prepares people for Rhodes Scholarships. You know those students, God bless them; I love them and I'm working with them too, but this is a time for active learning. This seems like a historical moment for it. And I guess that's where I see personally how my courses have changed, and inside I feel like the overall school is more and more committed to these active learning, engaged learning strategies that matter a lot. We're all catching up because our curriculum is still based on the old thing.

PART THREE

Adaptations

CHAPTER 3

Flying Solo

COLLECTIVELY OUR FACULTY STORIES attest to the essential elements of a faculty persona: curiosity, pursuit of new knowledge, and commitment to student learning and growth. Those are the constants. What has changed are what and how faculty teach and the certainty of how to make learning real for students. Within many of the stories we collected, there was a looming sense that while changes in the larger society come ever more rapidly, what lags behind, often dramatically, is the academy's response. It was the voice of a physicist near the end of his career that best captured this sense that what troubles faculty is not the inevitability of change but rather the absence of an understanding of how best to respond:

> In the university, education has changed dramatically over my lifetime in that when I began, universities were in many ways the sole repositories of large amounts of information, and that's no longer the case. There's plenty of information. The second function of universities was the training of students in how to reason and make advances with that knowledge and information. I don't feel like universities, even this one that claims to be a liberal arts university, have really made the change in themselves mentally that they no longer need to spend so much time and effort on knowledge and information; they need to put all of that energy into training students to use that information to do reasoning. Information is now cheap, but the reasoning is hard to do, hard to learn and expensive. And that's been an interesting change over my life. It's changed the way I've approached teaching quite a bit.

As students have changed in all kinds of ways, promoting, among other alterations, different pathways to learning, two fundamental insights become clear. First, teaching methods that once served an instructor well may no longer suffice to spur effective learning. Second, the traditional structures of the academy often impede the interdisciplinary learning on which the attainment of deep knowledge now increasingly depends. What will be required of many members of the academy going forward is a new willingness to move

beyond pedagogies that are as comfortable as they are familiar. For institutions, responding to change requires breaking through the boundaries that
confine knowledge to separate domains defined by discipline and department.
Increasingly, effective teaching necessitates moving beyond the precincts of
current pedagogical skills. At the institutional level, a faculty commitment to
teach—not just differently, but better—will require new, more open gateways
that allow creative thinking to range across standard disciplinary boundaries.

TEACHING MY WAY

Understanding how and why faculty teach requires first a recognition of
just how preemptive is the faculty's commitment to teaching courses of their
own design. What faculty want most is the freedom to organize the learning
process in ways that matter to them. In a way that few other professions allow,
collegiate teaching affords the opportunity to improve and grow by attempt-
ing different things, at different times, succeeding or failing, and learning from
the attempt. One of our storytellers put it this way:

> We're not a research institution, so I think what attracts faculty here and
> what keeps them here is a love of teaching, a love of learning, and a love of
> innovation. I could teach freshman biology wherever. I could stand up and
> spout my facts, close my book, and go to my office. What's the fun in that?
> And what's the fun in somebody handing me a class and saying, "Teach
> this"? I get some of my best ideas driving in here, and I'll change what
> we're going to do that day. We have the freedom to do that here. They also
> allow us to step out and see if something's going to work. We get to assess
> it: "Oh, that didn't work this semester; let's try something else." There are
> a lot of safety nets involved. Do we get bogged down in assessment? Yes.
> Do we get bogged down with student concerns? Yes. But isn't that what
> we're supposed to do? I think it does take someone who loves students.
> Learning. You have to be innovative. I am not teaching my classes the
> same way I taught them when I first started. I mean, how boring is that?
> Every so often, I just scrap something and do a totally new area in a class,
> and we can do that here as long as we're meeting the learning outcomes
> we've committed to accomplish with this class. So if I'm meeting a global
> literacy outcome, I can meet that in so many different ways. I'm going to
> try something new, and if that works, then I'll go to the faculty oversight
> group on global literacy and say, "OK, I think I want to change to this."
> They approve it, and then that becomes what we do for the next several
> semesters. So I think there's a lot of freedom.

Even as they celebrated the advances their students make in skills and
understanding, the teachers of undergraduates whose stories we collected

worried that good teaching is not a skill attained once and for all—it is not like learning to ride a bicycle. Rather it is a practice that requires continual revisiting, refreshment, and recasting. Understandably, then, faculty often give voice to the difficulty they encounter navigating changes that occur in the knowledge base and in their students' interests, goals, and learning styles. It is the instructor's job to define the content of a course, to define the cohort of students who should enroll based on their level of skill and advancement, and to define the methods of teaching employed:

> Right now, the mathematics faculty are in the middle of a massive change in how we handle developmental mathematics. What we recognized was that many students who normally enter developmental mathematics never pass it and never go on to complete their degrees. It really becomes a nail in the coffin for many students. We also know that a lot of students who get placed in developmental mathematics are misplaced. We have kids that take precalculus in high school that find themselves in developmental mathematics in college because they didn't score well on the placement test. So there are multiple strategies we're using right now to address that. One of the strategies I spearheaded is if students don't make the cutoff scores on the placement test, we place them straight into a college-level course based on their high school GPAs. Imagine if you're a strong student and took precalculus in high school, but then you're placed into arithmetic. What's your motivation level going to be like in your arithmetic class? We've been seeing students who say, "I know this stuff. This is dumb; this is boring; I'm bored." So they don't turn in their homework, and they don't pass, not because they lacked the aptitude to do well but because it's a mismatch for them. We piloted my idea this fall, and the anecdotal results were phenomenal in terms of success rates, with 80 to 90 percent of the students placed via this new method being successful. Once we do the formal statistical analysis, I'm anticipating that results will be so strong that we'll be able to cut the pilot short. This will mean that a lot of these students can be engaged in a higher-level course rather than be bored in the developmental math sequence . . . and we'll retain them better.

Faculty members often change the teaching methods and content of a course, not simply to stimulate their own interest, but also because the knowledge base itself has changed. In the case of this professor of environmental sciences, the teaching style and content have both undergone a complete transformation from the course of the same title he taught a quarter century ago:

> I worked in state government in Idaho for ten years and then came here. When I got here I had no idea there was a phrase called "active learning."

I didn't know what that was. My perspective was that I was terrified in the classroom. I had ten years' experience working in managing water quality for a state organization. I came to class and told people about it, and I tried to give them ideas about "If you leave this classroom and represent the state government for water quality management or USCP, you're going to be enforcing federal and state law to a bunch of people, some of whom don't want you to do that." This is how you get around all that; this is what you should do. And there was no active learning involved; it was just all kinds of stuff.

Now everything I do is active learning. Everything I do is case based, and it has been for a long, long time. One of my proudest student evaluations was when I had this whole page of all these questions, I asked, "I try to do these kinds of things in the classroom. What's your response to it?" Someone left the whole page blank and at the bottom, "You say it and I write it down; why can't you figure that out?" Because that ain't learning, that's why. So I teach with cases now. I teach with active learning now. It's writing intensive now. So they write papers about trying to be thoughtful about water quality management.

The field of water quality is completely different today from 1972 when I started teaching. It was a very gradual evolution, because I don't change very quickly. But it's a whole lot different now than it was when I started. My class is different every year. I re-create the class every year. I mean, "re-create" is a broad statement; I don't really do that. But I change it significantly every year because of new knowledge, new learning objectives, and all kinds of things.

The shift here is to employ content in the form of not textbooks but accounts that present the relevant facts as stories, whether derived from published cases or data from the students' own work in the field. Though the discipline is grounded in the natural sciences, the method of teaching comes to resemble a style more commonly associated with the humanities and social sciences—discussions based on narrative accounts of what it means to carry out policy mandates to ensure public health.

Reflecting more on how the changed external context has impacted what faculty members do in the classroom, another faculty member in physics spoke of his colleague:

The only way one professor I know can teach is to lecture, but he is a very inspiring person in the way he does it and creates an environment where learning is likely to happen. He provides sufficient inspiration to the students so that they can go home and do learning. The learning is something the kids have to do. The faculty can't do it for them. For a while, we all had to lecture. It was more or less a religion or a cult or something and we're finally moving away from that place. We're starting to understand that the students are human beings that have their own behaviors and foibles, just as the faculty do. For some faculty, lecturing is the best way to provide a learning environment. Others go completely the opposite way. The only people who upset me are the faculty that haven't even thought about their responsibility to create an environment where learning is likely to happen, and I would say the majority are like this. At this school, there's a strong minority that has a passion to try and find a sweet spot for them where their students are maximizing their learning. That's a very nice environment, I'd have to say.

There were also instances in which our faculty storytellers described changes in the physical environment—in their own rooms—that redefined the relationship of faculty to students. One professor described the time structural changes that were made to eliminate any suggestion of there being a "head" of the room as a professor's space and to place the instructor in a common realm, which was neither elevated nor otherwise privileged from the space that students inhabited:

> The provost who was here at the school for a hot minute was really interested in my work and said, "If you could really do what you wanted, what would it be?" I said, "Oh, I'd have a design-intensive workshop with faculty and completely redesign some of the first-year courses so they were project based." So she built me a room for $250,000 that has floating furniture, lots of tech, and no front. That was the thing, I said, "I wanted no front to the room."
>
> The provost's and the chancellor's office together provided me with more budget to run a set of redesigned interdisciplinary first-year courses. For instance, I have a political science and an English class. I have a science and an English class. I've got a multicultural and gender studies and communications class. The faculty redesigned those courses and moved away from lecture. They can flip them if they want to, but really they don't seem to do that. Instead, they privilege literacy practices, where the reading becomes more important and there's more work in and out of class to support it. The students work on projects, and all those classes have to have a public component, which is one of the design constraints.

I AND MY STUDENTS

Everywhere we interviewed them, faculty talked of their universal passion for teaching. It is a commitment that extended not just to the subject matter but also to students' success in learning. While they take justifiable pride in contributing to students' advancements as they occur, faculty members understand the continuing need to explore and develop their own teaching, both to retain their own freshness and to address changing student interests. Faculty members, principally as individuals, are discovering that the transition from teaching well to teaching better entails moving beyond reliance on a pedagogy that has become familiar and comfortable:

> The part that I really love about directing the Faculty Development Center is that you don't have to sell anybody that walks through the door that there's a problem with student learning. They've already decided that there is, so the first step, which is the hardest, has been done for me, but they give a variety of reasons for the problem. Some of them identify the problem as a student problem. "My students come to me, and they're unprepared." "My students come to me and they're not ready to learn." "My students don't pay attention." Some of them perceive the problem as being structural. "In my program, students don't have this prerequisite that they really need before they take this class." I also have people that are very upfront that they are not the teacher that they want to be or know that they should be. And that's a startling admission.

Yet "out with the old, in with the new" is not everyone's rallying cry. A variety of faculty from different kinds of institutions and a variety of disciplines spoke of retaining their investment in the lecture as a method of teaching that requires their students to develop their own ways of thinking and their own understanding of the spaces in which their learning takes place. A telling insight from one story is that the time that professors share with their students ought to be regarded as a special opportunity and as time to be used well:

> I bring up with new faculty the idea that they have to consider the time with the student to be special. If you're just standing there talking at them and giving them stuff they can learn from a book or from viewing a slide set or some things online, you're not taking full advantage of this opportunity, which is to get students to look, to see you, work with you, work with each other, and actually learn and apply what they're learning. And so, flipping the classroom these days is one of the things I've been pushing as a really good idea. And I think there are ways that you can put quality learning or teaching online too, totally online.
>
> When you take these different approaches to teaching students, it's not just other faculty who are resistant; it's the students who are almost the most resistant. There are ways around that, and in fact these days it's becoming easier. When we first started doing this in the late nineties, the

students were militantly resisting it. What we would do is just start the class and say, "This is unlike other classes. We are going to expect this from you. We're going to have these kinds of interactions. You have to come prepared. We are not going to act as the experts. We're not going to just stand here and fill your brain. That's not what we're here for. We believe you bring very important information to this class, and we believe that we bring important information, and we're going to see how these combine." So we set it up, and I had no problem saying, "And if that doesn't feel comfortable to you, you can drop this course. But you're going to be expected to do this."

Now students are much more used to doing group work and to doing more of this interactive stuff. They still do prefer to be fed. I think that is one of the other things that faculty who are resistant or reluctant, let's say, find intimidating to do is to break the class of that. And there are ways to do it, and you have to do it right away, the first day or two.

It's really key that the instructor models this. I find myself all the time breaking back into my lecturing mode, and so I have to catch myself and say, "That was five minutes of lecture. That's not what we're going to do anymore here. We're going to . . . and you're letting me, so you're actually enabling me." I turn it on the students. I think this will continue to be an issue, because it's easier for students to come to a class and just sit there and take whatever in they want to take in.

I would also set up things in my courses where students had to essentially do readings or preparation beforehand and then take (and this is what I liked about some of the online things) an online quiz before the class started to make sure that they had read it. I called these learning readiness quizzes. I would have online the reading or the outline or whatever it was for the lecture for the day. They had to read it and take the quiz online, and then I closed it so as soon as the class started, they couldn't take the quiz anymore. I then had them get in their groups and retake the quiz as a group. What I found, as you might expect, is that the average on the quizzes was 75 percent or 70 percent for the individuals, but when I had them retake the quiz as groups, the average was 95. After that I would say, "You all learn from each other because the quiz shows that now you at least as a group collectively understand this stuff at a high level. So that's where I'm starting, and that is where we will go. And that's where our projects begin because I know you know this stuff now."

Another faculty member, reflecting on a professional career in which lecturing has provided a special means for engaging his students, explained that, for him, lectures have never been simple recountings of the information that students can garner from reading the assigned texts. The lecture is rather an exercise that reinforces a faculty member's freedom to explore questions that arise from a life of continuous reading and thinking not just within but also around the field of study. Lecturing has been an act to expand the domain of learning beyond familiar boundaries:

> I mean, lecture courses have their own raison d'être. It's like thinking that books are a heavy price to pay for a lot of sound bites put together. I know that what I always tried to do in the lectures was to take one problem that was a conjunction of a literary and often a technical problem and a larger historical issue. Say, how does free verse work in Whitman and what is the possible relationship to a democratic culture? Or the multiplot in Dickens, and the creation of metropolises or the stream of consciousness in *Ulysses* and advertising? So I always try to join something that was hyperliterary, often very technical. You know, stream of consciousness—how exactly does this work? Why are there no verbs, et cetera? What does advertising mean in terms of experience, of objects, of money, et cetera, et cetera? But in these matters, I'm an anarchist. I think that departments ought to have good rules for people to coexist with each other but then should let people feel free to go.

This professor also posed a contrarian view that giving a lecture and learning from a lecture ought to be celebrated as a core pedagogical skill and decidedly not a method of teaching to be carelessly disparaged:

> I think—and you can put this in writing—in fact, I would love for you to put this in writing. I think that the exaggerated reliance of American universities on the seminar system is a very big mistake. Learning to sit at a lecture and learning from a lecture is an intellectual ability that students should be taught. In a place like this, and in many other places in the U.S., if we could teach everything through seminars, people would be happy to do that—both teachers and students. I think that's a mistake. Teachers ought to lecture because that's intellectual discipline for us. And students ought to listen to lectures because that's intellectual discipline for them as well.
>
> You know, I come from a different culture. In my home country, when I finished university, there were no PhDs. So at twenty-two, if you were lucky, you got some kind of a grant of sorts, which is what I got. And basically, they opened a door and said, "Go in and teach." And there were two hundred people there and you are to lecture. And so you had to learn how to lecture. So that is the first thing. I mean, lecturing is a skill. And the skill has very little to do with the little jokes and the little things. In

this country, it's a skill, but it's not really taught because so much relies on seminars. At this point, large lecture courses in the States are considered to be an inevitable price to pay for lack of resources. And I think that's wrong.

Some of the more compelling accounts we heard were of faculty members who had begun their careers by lecturing and found that students frankly were not paying attention and could not conceive what possible importance the subject might have in their lives, even as majors. One young faculty member told of her transformation from an ineffective lecturer to one who came to invest a dry subject matter with elements that piqued student interest in a remarkable way and, in the process, came to redefine her own responsibilities:

I was teaching introductory cell biology, and students just did not know how this information fit in. They would come and ask me questions; it would just drive me crazy. It's like, "Is this going to be on the exam?" And now looking back, I realized what they were saying was "I have no earthly idea why anyone would care about this. What would this be useful for? Why does it matter?" No frame of reference. Subsequent to that, like many, at least scientists, I went in and I just started teaching. I didn't learn about the psychology of learning, even though it's a biological process, and so I didn't even honestly realize that to make a memory, you have to actually activate circuits that are already up there.

I was very naïve, but I was frustrated because, first I thought, "What's wrong with these students?" And then I would have conversations with them, and I realized, you know, it kind of is my job to make something interesting. I thought before it's not my job; they should be interested in this stuff. My job is just to deliver the facts or get them to know the facts. Anyway, I was trying to think of what I could do that would just automatically help students understand why cell biology matters. And so I thought, well, diseases are a good thing. I looked for a disease that had aspects of genetics; it had aspects of cell structure, function, and aspects of all the different topics that I could imagine. The idea that I had was to use the disease kind of as a back and forth for the course and as the common example that we'd keep coming back to.

The very first course is the story of the day that the girl, Alex, died. After telling the story, I would say, "Alex died of a disease called cystic fibrosis, and if we could just get that protein to the surface, we could actually cure almost everyone with cystic fibrosis. So we're going to start with the plasma membrane and the function of the plasma membrane." I used that to keep coming back to. I don't know how effective it was; I didn't measure; I wasn't an education researcher, but all I know is that they never asked, "Is this going to be on the exam or why do I need to know it?" So it solved a problem that I had.

I think at that point, I began to think of my role differently. I had said, "It's not my job to spoon-feed them; it's not my job to get them interested. That's their job." But I started to realize that it actually was my job and that the better I did that, the better they'd be able to learn it. That's been a transition for me. Yes, we are advocates, not only for our subject matter, but also for higher education, for engaged citizenship, for all of the things that the academy represents.

Those kinds of successes made me define my role as a teacher more broadly. I didn't even read the education literature; I didn't know that it existed. It was kind of approaching the classroom like it's a science experience. It's like I have this problem. Maybe if I do this, it will solve it. And then slowly I learned more and more. I learned there is a literature out there; there are all of these kinds of approaches. Of course, I didn't invent them, but somehow I needed to reinvent them because I didn't know where to find them. There was no mechanism that was available to me then. It was before I got tenure, so this was pretty early on in my academic career.

There are two lessons: my job is broader as a teacher than I had ever envisioned, and it's not honestly about the content. It's about what students do with the content. It is my job to figure out ways to invite them into that content, to welcome them into it in a way that lets it connect. Otherwise, it's just going to drip right through. They're never going to remember. It's going to go right through.

In Pursuit of Better Teaching

Such progress, however, is seldom easy. The first sticking point is often the accreditor's and hence the administration's promotion of a whole new set of assessment practices designed to document the learning that occurs in classrooms. This story reflects a quite simple lesson: that if the assessment of learning is unfamiliar or threatening to faculty members, the likelihood is that they will resist incorporating the new practices intended to help instructors better understand what their students are learning. The institutional challenge most administrations face is the need to have faculty see assessment as a process providing concepts and methods that yield a better understanding of how well their students are learning—and, when necessary, concrete plans for changing curriculum and teaching methods to yield better learning in their own classes:

We don't have assessment police here. I see myself as a champion of assessment, but I have to do it within the confines of my own teaching. It's a very sensitive issue because this is a responsibility that people feel very strongly as being imposed on them, as being an additional workload, and if they don't buy into it, that it's at the heart of student learning, then typically the rationale is that this is just for accreditation, and therefore it's not significant.

Our council is generating conversations and resources for people to learn more about assessment. The research indicates that the lack of knowledge of assessment is a real barrier for faculty. Some of us come to it really easily because it's like organizational evaluation, evaluation of programs and of outcomes. That's a comfort zone for me. This is also not hard for people who do evaluative research, but for other people it is, number one. And number two, it's just not within their comfort zone for faculty to admit that they don't know how to do something. They are more likely to just do it and make it look like it's supposed to look. So the conversations my council has [with faculty] are really for encouraging people to consider resources, to look at what they're doing, and to give them affirmation.

This tale lays the groundwork for another dimension of teaching better. Ultimately, the transition from one stage of teaching to another works best when more than a few individual faculty members or isolated clusters are involved. Teaching better ultimately comes to thrive on the commitments that faculty make not just to themselves but to colleagues and academic partners as well. For tenured faculty especially, no administration can mandate adoption of a particular teaching method or practice. Administrators concerned with their own survival know well that mandates are seldom if ever successful in changing faculty behavior. As a matter of principle, most faculty members will resist any exhortation to change unless it seems within their own interest to do so. One of our faculty conversations included a description of a former mentor who had served as dean of a major academic unit of a large institution. When asked once how he had achieved such remarkable success in changing the culture of his faculty, he replied, "Quite simple—in my first year, I took one hundred people out to lunch."

Instilling a culture of teaching better very often requires this kind of one-on-one approach. Individual conversations can sometimes help one who is reluctant to realize that what had seemed foreign or threatening is really not so different from one's own thinking and practice. In this example, a faculty member discovered that the barrier to buying in had simply been a matter of language:

We have a capstone in chemistry where students do a research project for one semester, and there is a creativity outcome associated with all the

capstones. I really did not get how to make an assignment that demonstrated the creativity outcome. My course got recalled, and I knew I didn't
meet the criteria, so I went to the head of the creativity roundtable. We
sat down together, and we talked about it. What he said to me was, "You
really need to think of this not as creativity but as innovation." And then it
all made sense to me, right, because I'm a science person. When he put
it in the words of "think of it as innovation," well, I know all about innovation. So that made it easy, and it really clicked when I redid the research
assignment.

Our travels to collect faculty stories reinforced our sense that the cultures of institutions—and of individual departments within institutions—vary
greatly. Some exhibit a willingness of individual faculty members to step
beyond the realm of individual independence in order to act in ways that
improve learning for an entire department. One heartening example is from
the community college we visited:

> Some of the most impactful changes from our cooperative learning move-
> ment have been in the math department here. We are a very collaborative
> group, which is having an effect on all of our math students. There are
> other divisions where there is a lot of, I would say, infighting. There
> are seven of us in our department, and there have been times when
> we've even made personal sacrifices as far as giving up seniority levels and
> things like that to say, "No, you go ahead," just for the greater good. This
> attitude is really reflected in the success of our math students overall. We
> all really do want them to succeed. Sure, we have people on this side, and
> we have people on that side personality-wise, but deep down, we know
> that each one of us is very dedicated to our students. We know that. It's
> very organic.
>   We take seriously the idea that the purpose of negotiation is to deal
> with the issue. You attack the issue, not the people, and I think we just
> have a good group when it comes to that. We deal with the issue, and
> we don't attack people's personalities or the people themselves because we
> know at heart, they have good intentions.

More often, however, the prevailing instinct remains one of self-
preservation. As in the story that follows, the instinct is to build the fortress
that defines and protects one's own courses or department. The teller also
hints that, whatever benefits it might confer to the major, turf protection
among departments generally does not serve the interest of students:

> There are two things that we do here. There's a Friday forum where
> people present some things that they're doing in the classroom or their

research and there are also luncheons that are put together by the associate provost. We have lunch together one Thursday a month, and we share ideas. Like this one: on a committee, we're piloting a new active learning classroom, which ties into another school here. I'm really interested in that. How can the institution support us with space where we can apply what we're doing across departments and across divisions?

This college, however, is built on the logic of departments that depart from each other. We teach our students how one topic departs from another. The type of education that most interests me is one that creates experiences that confuse those boundaries and that fuse those boundaries, experiences that don't focus so much on how we depart from each other but more on how we might overlap and combine and commingle.

Other portraits revealed how the academy itself has become partitioned in ways that prevent what could conceivably become a natural infusion of skills and ways of thinking exhibited in other disciplines. A testimonial of this kind serves as a reminder of the fact that the academy has evolved considerably from the earlier conception of preparing students for life by engaging them substantially with knowledge from several fields. Though the research degree continues to be denoted as doctor of philosophy, most teacher-scholars who have earned this degree are no longer "philosophers" in the early sense of having studied and learned broadly across a spectrum of knowledge. What seems at stake in the behavior as described here is not so much how well students might learn as which department should have primary ownership of a skill to be developed. Turf matters:

Who naturally teaches most of the writing for the first-year seminar? Right, the English department has a huge role in that, as you would imagine. If we're going to turn away from relying on English faculty as much as we are right now, that creates a huge problem for them in terms of workload, in terms of perception on campus among our colleagues. And there are a lot of problems with this type of thinking where turf is getting in the way. I feel that this is our most important program, because it's our students' first introduction to college. This is where we state what we're all about. Why wouldn't we have the absolutely best faculty teaching this? The most dynamic, the most elegant, the most inspiring people, regardless of what discipline they teach, regardless of frankly even how well they teach the skill of writing. I can learn the pedagogy in writing. We're all smart people around here, right? What I can't learn is how to connect with students in a very personal way, with that kind of classroom dynamism that you see when someone walks in and just gives a million-dollar lecture and you sit back and go, "That was amazing." We've all been to that lecture, or at least I hope we've all been to that lecture. I get chills when I think about the lectures I had in medieval music, which is dry as white toast, but that professor of mine would come in without notes, and he would sing passages without score. I mean, this guy was amazing. He was absolutely amazing. And that's the kind of guy you want to teach in a first-year seminar, right? And instead, we worry about whether the faculty in the English department will lose turf if they don't teach writing.

Another story offers a modest proposal that one might think makes perfect sense from the standpoint of engaging several related disciplines in designing a common introductory course sequence and from the standpoint of realizing some efficiencies in the delivery of such courses. The proposal begins with an observation about how curriculum generally gets created and developed in higher education:

We have an immature curriculum system, built around the notion of accumulation. It's like a really bad shopping list or scavenger hunt. Get two of these things, get three of these. It's an accumulation model, and we're trying to move towards a progress model.

People are starting to realize that you need to start thinking about learning this way, but even if we had a technological tool right now that had all the features available to us, we wouldn't have what we need to punch into that tool because we haven't worked out the logic of our own sequences yet, because we never had to. We treated it as "pick one of these seventy-three." The joke I repeatedly make at presentations is if you had looked five years ago at the enrollment numbers of our top twenty courses without any other information, you'd think we were a seminary school because we had an insane number of students taking History of World Religions because it picked up four gen ed tags. Then somebody came along and said, "No class can have that many gen ed tags." They pulled back, and now this course has settled back to being just another amongst the humanities offerings. But we had this insane spike where we had literally thousands of students taking history. We had to scramble to find adjunct faculty. The Philosophy and Religious Studies Department went from being a philosophy department with a few religious studies faculty to being a religious studies department with a few philosophy faculty. If you build that kind of accumulation model where you treat everything as equivalent, that's where you end up unless you put some other kind of check on it.

In contrast to that, I use the idea of imagining a six-lane highway. Each lane is a broad category like medical, biological, and I can take gen ed classes that apply to everything that's within that broad path. I might take a basic biology class. If I decide that I'm going to do veterinary science instead of nursing assistant, I'm still good, right? And then gradually I'm able to narrow down into working with human beings versus working with animals, so I need anatomy and physiology. We're going to have to start talking about this idea that similar disciplines would have at the very beginning of their pathways classes that would work for all of their disciplines. So that's going to involve a lot of different thinking than what we have historically been asked to do. That makes a lot of people very uncomfortable. Some people get very excited; other people get frightened; other people get apprehensive. It's a big conversation that is going to be ongoing.

Viewing the introductory-level curriculum as a six-lane highway moving in a common direction, offering courses that satisfy the early learning requirements of several departments, could be the antidote to the accumulation model that more often prevails in higher education. It is hard to believe, though, that many departments would embrace this concept, for the simple reason that introductory courses are sources of enrollment and hence of revenue and justification for faculty lines. To be sure, the case against a curriculum interstate highway would not be mounted overtly along these lines but rather in intellectual terms stressing the need to preserve the integrity of the disciplines by tailoring instruction to students even in the very earliest stages of their exposure to the field. Yet the enrollment and financial subtext of these debates would be foremost in the minds of all those who care about maintaining the continued existence of their own department and their own jobs. For that reason, the accumulation model continues to prevail despite the escalation of costs, and it fortifies the instinct of departments to "depart" from the rest of the academy for purposes of self-justification and survival.

Faculty members understand very well the nature of the institutions they inhabit. Many can articulate how the structures of their institutions are less than optimal for instilling student learning in efficient or effective ways. For all that, there are comparatively few occasions in which reforming the curriculum or teaching is initiated and then sustained by the faculty of a university or college.

There are, to be sure, exceptions scattered across the landscape of American higher education. Over the course of our story collecting, we became acquainted with one institution in which the faculty had taken charge of both the curriculum and the assessment of student learning. It is a process begun some twenty years ago that continues to evolve. The story begins with faculty receiving a strong nudge from the administration, saying that to remain financially viable, the institution needed to develop a more compelling curriculum as a means to achieve distinctiveness in the student market. The clear message was that curriculum needed to change, and one of the tactics to deliver this message was the enactment of a funerary ritual for putting to rest those parts of the old curriculum whose time had passed:

> Have you heard the story of what happened when one of the assistant deans brought a coffin in to our faculty institute and announced the death of the old curriculum? I would say the overall reaction was negative; there was a lot of surprise, but nobody walked out. I think all of us were like, "What's next?" Next, they handed out three-by-five index cards and asked us to write things that we thought were wrong with the old curriculum. We were supposed to read them and throw them in the coffin. Some people actually participated in that; others of us said, "You've got to be kidding." I will give them credit for one thing—they did recognize that they couldn't create the curriculum and say this is what it will be. What they did do next is say, "You're the faculty, you need to create the curriculum." We were at that point divided into committees and were essentially told, "You're the experts, and so you guys have to devise the curriculum. The first thing you have to decide is, 'What does an educated college student look like?' Once that is decided, 'All right, how do you get there?'" And that was from ground zero.
>
> This was a very long process. There is no doubt about it. Years. It really took years. And it's still going on. Was it Twain—I forget—who basically said something about a camel being a horse designed by a committee? We're there now, because it's gotten to the point where it's good. It needs to be stopped being tinkered with except when it's fine-tuned tinkered.

It did take a long time, but it is a case in which the faculty collectively designed a curriculum that is a responsible and sincere attempt to teach students not just well, but better. The learning design includes a set of faculty review processes to monitor both new and existing courses to ensure that they fulfill the learning objectives that the faculty as a whole committed itself to achieve for its students. In the decades since the new curriculum was designed and implemented, the composition of the faculty has undergone a nearly complete turnover. Yet it remains an example of a faculty-designed curriculum that the current generation of faculty continue to support and deliver.

DRAWING THE LESSONS

Our gallery of vignettes attests to the things that faculty members care about as teachers of students, members of individual departments and disciplines, and citizens of their institutions. Collectively their stories reflect a commitment to a faculty profession as well as to the continued learning and growth of their students. Many perceive changes in their students, which often stir an awareness of the need to change their teaching.

As members of institutions, faculty often envision changes to the curriculum and to organizational structures that could result in better teaching and better learning—including some steps that could yield greater efficiency and reduced costs to their institutions. Our faculty storytellers were often astute analysts and critics of their institutions. As we have seen, they enjoy the academic freedom to design courses in ways that speak to their own proclivities and strengths. They often express anxiety and frustration that they are creatures of institutional and professional cultures that can hinder connections between branches of knowledge, often stressing proprietary claims that divide knowledge and learning into fortified and often contending departments. Most faculty affirm that they and their departments are capable of teaching well. While there are expressions of desire to teach better, many come to feel that the institutions they inhabit—and help shape—too often hinder their ability to achieve the improvements they envision.

The barriers to constructive change cause many faculty members to retreat into the relative sanctity of teaching their own classes as the one part of their professional lives over which they have direct control. This kind of personal emphasis also offers respite from the increasingly frenetic and overwhelming pace of their own lives and their institutions. Some thoughtful voices have articulated concerns that the growth of expectations and profusion of busyness have themselves come to detract from the quality of teaching and learning that occurs in their institutions. One of those faculty members advocated "slow learning" as an antidote to the preoccupation with speed at the expense of genuine, deep learning in students. His words offer a fitting close to this chapter:

> I've been playing with an idea that I just call simply "slow learning." I make an analogy between the slow food movement, which is about counteracting fast food, and academia, and I talk about how we could deliberately say "less is more." Less on the syllabus, maybe less requirements, students doing less things, less meeting. We could embrace a different pace, a slower pace that we do when we're at our best. "Slow learning" is part of a broader conversation about how to bring the human being back into academia. I'll put it that way. We've all become way too functional, and we have lost sight of what should be the humanism at the center of what we do. I'm very concerned about that, and I hope eventually our curriculum reflects the urgency of not only slowing down but of bringing human beings back again to the very center of what we do.

Faculty Voice

PRACTICE MAKES PERFECT

This professor worries that his undergraduate students lack sufficient writing skills to prepare them for a wide range of professional tasks. With the aid of a teaching assistant paid for out of his own pocket, he experimented with approaches until he felt that he finally reached the right balance of strong learning outcomes and teaching efficiency.

Traditionally my Spanish section in the Department of International Languages, Literatures, and Cultures has been really literature-heavy. All except for one of us faculty members were PhD students of literature and Latin American studies or literature and Spanish. One linguist, the rest literature. You know how it is. The message you get in graduate school is this is what's intrinsically important. This is what everybody needs to study.

I became increasingly concerned about how our program was preparing students to write essays and whether or not they'd be able to transfer those skills into some other profession. So I decided over last summer that I was going to redesign Spanish 301, which is reading and composition. I got help from a student, who I then hired to be my T.A. in the fall, to completely redo the course based on skills needed in any job: reading the kinds of things that you need to be able to read just in your life and in your job and writing the kinds of things that you need to be able to write well.

I also thought that I'd design the course to be so student centered that the students themselves would answer a survey on the first day and that I would choose readings on the basis of the topics they chose in the survey. My T.A. and I were completely crazy. We were way overly ambitious in how we redesigned the class, and yet we learned a lot that first semester.

We had to pull back a little bit and do another redesign for the spring, and this semester I'm very happy with the class. The students have four low-stakes writings from three drafts to two required drafts. On the first day, they handwrite a paper. This is very interesting. It's the first time that I've gone back to in-class writing being handwritten. I'd gone really all electronic. You know, why waste the paper? They're used to it. Since we're teaching them to write in a different language, however, they were using the spell-check and dictionaries way too heavily and not even using them well.

I gave them extensive feedback on their strengths and weaknesses on their first papers from that first day. Then I made them get into groups based on strengths and weaknesses. Every group had to have all of the strengths covered, which included critical thinking, creativity, organization, spelling, accents, sophistication of grammar, all those kinds of things. Based on their strengths, they're required to give five concrete examples or suggestions for improvement to each of their group members.

After these group sessions, they're required to turn in on time something that includes all of the bottom-line criteria that must be in their writing. They have to give feedback to all of their peers and then turn in a final version, which addresses all of the comments made by their peers. They can also come see me during my office hours and meet with the T.A.—who did really well in my class last semester—who I'm paying out of my pocket. I'm trying to focus on writing as a process, so some of them end up having to write four or five drafts and some of them end up having two drafts. They decide.

Now we're going into the email writing segment. My wife had this idea. She was saying how she really wished somebody had taught her to write a professional email. During the first class, I asked for a raise of hands on how many people had an automatic signature that they could apply to their emails. Only three out of twenty have that. And nobody had ever written a professional email with all of the elements that are pointed out in the two articles that I gave them on how to write a professional email. This is immediate learning that is immediately applicable.

Interestingly enough, the feedback I got from last semester was that having students choose their own topics was a failure. Both the T.A. and the students said that. There was too little coherence, and it was so much work for me to try to get all of those different readings based on the different topics. Insane, insane, yeah. So I learned that from their feedback, plus what did the students engage with most? Well, aside from the reading in the one field they chose, it was literature. Literature is what they engage with, so I can use it as the wonderful humanistic learning tool that it is without it being about analyzing literature as literature. It could be more cultural. All of this feedback from last semester has made this semester really, really better, and I now also believe that with the number of e-quizzes I've got and the extra structure that I've put in, this course is superefficient. Finally.

Faculty Voice

BEING A DOULA

Some faculty members told us stories about how real-life experience changed how they engaged their students. The teller of this story, an adjunct professor of architecture, shares how her engaging a doula to help with her third pregnancy opened her eyes to the possibility of playing a similar role for architectural students as they prepared their final projects and their walk through "the valley of despair" that was part of the drama of their presentations.

I have three children, and I had a doula for my third child, thought about it for the second child, so I'm familiar with that role. The idea is that whereas a midwife is there to deliver a baby, a doula is there to support the mom, both during the pregnancy, during the birth, and afterwards.

We tend to have around forty to forty-five graduate students, and each of them is working either with an individual faculty or with a studio instructor. That studio instructor is really more the midwife who is there to help them deliver the project, right? And the studio instructor and the student have a particular relationship in that the student makes the work and the studio instructor is the critic who gives the feedback. The critic ultimately provides a pass/fail grade.

What I decided to do was to become a doula, and a doula is first of all available to all students across the sections. On the one hand, there is a logistical studio coordinator component to my role, but I also meet with students. It is sort of like a counseling role. I ask them a question, I listen to them for a really long time, and then I basically throw back what I hear but with just enough reframing that they kind of go, "Ohhhh!" The role is really about helping them clarify what it is that they're doing and helping them present their work in the best light.

I also play a doula supportive role to both students and faculty by interpreting. When a student becomes frustrated with a faculty member, I'm able, first of all, to sometimes bring that information back to the faculty or back to the head as needed, but I mainly help the student interpret what the faculty member means and/or what the architecture faculty more broadly is looking for in terms of expectations. Because I'm not the one directly evaluating their project and I'm not the one responsible for grading them, it is just a more open relationship.

What I'm finding is that this sort of role means that I have a really important responsibility to be careful about how I'm exchanging information, right? It can be really easy to feel casual with students and want to tell them stuff that you know from a faculty meeting and vice versa. So I need to be very careful about that relationship, yeah. It is, however, also important to the graduate program to have someone who is able to pull back and look across the work and who is able to say, "This student should connect with this student because their projects have some alignment, and this student should connect with this student." And "These are the things that we're seeing globally across the studio." That sort of oversight, I think, is important to the program.

The doula and the midwife meet on a regular basis. So again, part of the work is logistics. You have interim reviews that you have to schedule. You have to figure out who's going when and who are the guest critics coming in. We have periodic meetings with students about how they're doing and how they're progressing. Who are you concerned about? Who are you not? I have told students that invariably, every spring semester someone loses a very, very important relationship. We've had people who are going through divorce or separation, and they're trying to get their project done or some crisis has just happened, so there's a confidential conversation about when and where you give somebody slack or how do you support them.

There's also this phenomenon called "the valley of despair," and I've told students I rarely see anybody get through a master's final project without hitting the valley of despair. The important thing is to recognize that you can and will get through it. But I'm the one who can be there to help them get through the valley of despair. I'm thinking specifically right now of a student who needed to talk to me, and we went outside the building, and he just needed to cry. He just needed to release. That's part, again, of the counseling role, just being present and knowing they need to be heard. Even if I can't necessarily help them directly, if they're frustrated or confused, they just need to be heard.

My annual review is coming up next week, and I'm working on that prep. I was just looking at course evaluations this morning from last fall. And paraphrasing, one student said, "She masterfully balanced being empathetic and being firm and having high expectations and actually acknowledging that these are human beings that have lives and feelings and all that sort of stuff."

CHAPTER 4

Change Is All about Us

WHEN FACULTY TALK ABOUT change, their conversations are often vaguely apprehensive, as if acknowledging the line from Bob Dylan's "The Times They Are a-Changin'": "Your sons and your daughters / Are beyond your command." Change is everywhere—in students, in knowledge, in society. It is an imperative when it is not a distraction, a mystery that steadily unfolds, as the song says: "And don't speak too soon / For the wheel's still in spin." Most faculty encounters with change are personal, and as often as not, what comes across from their observations is that while they have changed, their students have changed even more—in ways that present challenges one would not likely have foreseen in earlier times.

A twelve-year veteran math teacher at a community college who spent a half dozen years as an adjunct before becoming a regular full-time faculty member says,

> So these are students who've just graduated from high school, and some of them have been out of school for a while, and we "placement test" everybody for math. So these students come in below college-ready. And they can be as below college-ready as needing basic arithmetic, which is essentially fifth-grade math, or they could wind up needing introductory algebra, which I guess you could call eighth-grade math.

But she is ready to soldier on, in search of common ground on which to build:

> I try to have conversations with a whole class of students by asking them questions like, "What do you imagine the future is going to be like? What are you going to use math for? Anybody have any ideas at all?" I'm amazed by how context-free some of my students are, especially the younger ones. It's virtually impossible to have a discussion about even a simple concept like ratio or proportion with a modern high school graduate. You ask, "Didn't you ever make a model?" And they look at you: "No." "Did you ever make cookies, the slice-and-bake ones?" "No." "Where you have to

actually mix the stuff up?" "No." OK, how do I teach them proportion if they've never done it? You find yourself saying, "A map? You've read a map, haven't you? The paper maps that have a scale on them?" No, wait a minute. They just pinch and zoom and they change the scale at a moment's notice. So when do they do proportional reasoning? The scale is whatever they want it to be. It's really a challenge sometimes for faculty to take the material and contextualize it so that they can see how to use it. That's my objective. I know there are these competencies I have to hit and all, but I want them to be able to do something useful with what they're learning. Not everybody's going to be an engineer or an accountant, but I want them to be able to handle finances and to listen to a politician and decide, "No, that's bogus; that doesn't make any sense." Right? Everybody has to do that, and it's a challenge sometimes. It really is. Part of it is modern life. You realize how old you are when you think, "Oh, my gosh! I did build models. I played with Tinkertoys!"

Finding Common Ground

The stories told about students often reflect this sense of disconnect between faculty and student experiences. The next account makes clear that teaching German in a liberal arts college is no easier than teaching math in a community college. And while there are some strategies to engage and connect with students in the introductory classes, they become harder to sustain in higher-level classes:

> As a teacher, I want to continually get better, and I like to understand my students, but that goal keeps moving. I think the students are slightly different today than they were even twelve years ago when I started here. I don't know how much you can expect them to read outside in their free time or even to watch movies. There are just so many ways in which I realize I'm not the same as they are.
>
> The presentation matters. Yeah, it's true, you have to try to meet them where they are, and where they are is not necessarily doing worksheets or just reading. You have to be interactive and entertaining, which is actually a little exhausting at times, but it's exciting to have that challenge of, "How can I meet these people? I know this stuff is great and fascinating and interesting and useful. How can I make sure that they get that?" The beauty of teaching 100-level, courses in particular, is that you can revert a bit to childhood and play "Head, Shoulders, Knees, and Toes" in German. But for more advanced topics, I don't have that same bag of tricks.

We have a colleague, Joan Girgus, who was dean of the College and chair of the Psychology Department at Princeton. She would occasionally observe that, too often, faculty wanted their students to be like them. What a travesty that would be, she would then conclude, if the whole world looked like the small percentage of the population who became scholars/teachers. In fact, most faculty know well that a comparatively small number of students will pursue their own devoted paths to advanced study; at the same time, they feel it is not asking too much of students to take the classroom experience seriously—to set aside distractions and focus on the matter at hand as the common ground between professor and student:

> I have a group of nine or ten students in my study jam where we study for two hours at a clip. There's a student peer mentor who really leads the group, but then the faculty is there to add some gravitas maybe and just to show that faculty are approachable. It's a great group. Everybody has a laptop, and they're doing a lot of their work online, but they've got three or four screens open. They're supposedly studying, but they're also doing all these other things. I see this in the classroom too. Everybody has head-phones on or little earbuds. One young woman was obviously listening to music, supposedly reading, and she's kind of bopping like this. I said, "OK, you can't really be concentrating if you're singing along to this thing and bopping." After this incident, the student mentor and I made a rule that we weren't going to be listening to anything for one study jam a week, even though some of them said, "I have to listen to music in order to study." "Well, we're going to try it without music."

On Media, Communication, and Expectations

In part—but only in part—technology is the villain. Too much, too fast, too inexplicable. More than that, technology changes not just the means but the conventional forms of communication as well. For faculty who believe in teaching students how to organize, structure, and then communicate what they have learned, the opportunities for a teachable moment are nearly endless:

> We have students who come in and don't understand how to write. They do creative writing without punctuation and sentence structure. They say, "That's fine." And I say, "But it's not fine." I get emails that start with "Hey." I respond and say, "Sorry, that's not my name. When you struc-ture a proper email to me, I'll be glad to address your issues." It's one of those teachable moments. I'm trying to teach them that this is the kind of response they'll get when they need something. If they don't put their request in a proper framework and form, they won't get what they need or want.

Even as they feel challenged by the infusion of technology in their students' lives, faculty across the spectrum of institutions we visited talked readily about how the availability of digital tools has affected their interactions with their students. The following reflection pays tribute to the expanded possibilities that digital media afford. Accompanying this power, however, is a sense of ambivalence created by the heightened expectation of a timely response that is most often the rhythm of social media applications. The instructor is always on call. She loves teaching but notes the change in focus that has occurred:

I don't think technology was the driver for this change in focus, because nothing drives higher education more than faculty and administrators. You could, however, buy a simple little software program, for example, that allowed you to have group papers or people working on a project; you could see that digitally and you could give students feedback. That software was enabling you to become more student centered as opposed to more distant. When I was a student, I was using email for information but not as a regular tool, but since I've been here, this is the tool for communicating with your students. We might actually have fewer students in our office hours because we can answer more questions by email, but we're also doing that 24-7. That too makes us more accessible and a little bit more student centered, I think. So while the innovations of technology have kind of driven us, we still have a rubric expectation for an exemplary online class that requires "student-centered" contact or interaction of some form or fashion.

Many of the faculty conversations focusing on change—particularly on those changes that might be attributed to social media and related information technologies—reflected further ambivalence. It was as if the faculty member wanted to first assure his listener that his was not a calling being driven by technological change so that it would be safe to launch into a story about how technology was changing him and his students. At these moments, it helped to be a skeptic and something of a curmudgeon:

People are constantly talking about a new breed of student. There's no new breed of student. Yes, evolution is an ongoing process, but it proceeds at a really incredibly snail-slow pace. One of the most nonsensical terms in the world is multitasking. Insurance companies now charge teenage girls more money because they can't multitask and they walk into traffic and get hit while they're texting. Yeah, they're focused on the text; they're not focused on the walking. We can't multitask effectively. We make up things for each generation. When I was in college, it was all about individualized instruction. Then everything was going to be replaced by video class-rooms, and then everything was going to be replaced by distance learn-ing. Now we find out that the University of Phoenix can only graduate 20 percent of their students. Evolution has dictated mostly how human beings learn, and we need to recognize that as fact. Yes, it's great to take advantage of all the new technology. In fact, I just did a wonderful little PowerPoint demonstration in the class I came from right before I saw you. All right, but it's an accompaniment; it's an accessory. It's not the main strategy. What people have forgotten how to do is literally to talk to the students and tell them stories to keep them engaged. That's what's changed.

GOING THE EXTRA MILE(S)

For many of the faculty with whom we talked, this ambivalence derives not just from the changing modes of interaction with students but also from the amount of individual attention that many students need. On the one hand, there was a commitment to being helpful, while on the other, there was an exasperation with students who require what might seem like extraor-dinary levels of assistance. One might argue that teachers of any genera-tion commonly make these kinds of observations about their students. And while the sense of fulfillment in helping students reach their goals is timeless, the thought of needing to go multiple extra miles for more students can be daunting:

> Students today don't know how to transition from high school to college. It is extremely different. Not knowing study habits, not understanding they have to do homework. I think the school system is not preparing them for this, and I think maybe it's because I'm back in mentoring this year that I see it more collectively. They're still intelligent. It's that their work ethic is very different, a challenge I think we all face in higher education. I currently have one student who is easily distracted (that's a nice way to put it) by so many other things going on. I meet with him quite fre-quently and say, "OK, what can we do?" I met with him to talk about time management, and it seemed to help for a while, and then a distraction came along. I just keep pushing with him and trying. That's the only thing I can do.

> There's a big problem if a student isn't trying as hard as I am, but it's very easy to tell early on if this is the case. I will give you one example. We've had a student in our program who is a double major with art and is currently a senior. She has had ups and downs—health-related issues, issues with her sport; so she's had a lot of personal things going on. She

has just persevered. I had a conversation with her last year and said, "What do you want to do? What is your goal? What do you want to accomplish?" Once we had that conversation, she had a very set path, and she knew exactly what she needed to do in order to accomplish what she wanted. I gave her ideas of how to get there, and she's doing it now. One of my biggest success stories of recent years is to see her respond to that pushing and poking in a very positive way.

To be engaged, a student needs to be motivated—and there is the rub. Just how responsible is a teacher for doing more than providing guidance and encouragement? Is there an obligation as well to literally push the student up the mountain he says he wants to climb? It turns out, helicopter advisors may be no more acceptable than helicopter parents:

> I have a young gentleman struggling through precalc, for the third time, because he needs to have calculus to do prepharmacy, but he seems unwilling to commit to what's going to make him successful in precalc. I found out that he dropped it one time and he failed it the next time. So I told him this has got to be the final shot. I said, "What are we going to do to make sure that this time is different?" It's like he's playing the bench. I haven't seen any flags from him lately, and I think I probably should check in on him at a good point, but I don't want to be a helicopter advisor. I feel like these students aren't encouraged to be responsible for themselves enough, but maybe he's just incapable for some reason of being able to pass precalc. I mentioned to him, "There has to be a plan B or a plan C. Why don't you declare a biology major since you're leading in all those biology classes?" Yes, he's taken gen chem; he's taken organic; and yes, I don't think I've ever gotten a word of warning about those. But there obviously is a math issue, at least with precalc. And maybe he just doesn't really like it enough or isn't willing to bite the bullet, so to speak, to do what I guess I feel like successful students do—meaning they get in there and they ask for help.

The unvoiced question in this account is what level of intervention is suitable to motivate the student and who bears responsibility if the student fails. Does allowing an unmotivated student to fail teach a valuable life lesson, or does it solidify that student's consignment to constricting horizons and unfulfilled potential? As the critiques of higher education's less-than-optimal graduation rates coupled with its rising costs become more acute, faculty and other staff members may well ask, "Do we sell students down the river and solidify our failure to educate successfully if we withhold our utmost efforts to help them succeed?"

INFORMATION OVERLOAD AND STRESS

The other problem, beyond permanently distracted and disconnected students, is the sheer knowledge overload that the new information technologies facilitate for both students and faculty. It is exhausting: more to do, more to pay attention to, more demands for nearly instantaneous responses. The challenge faculty often face daily involves not just making students aware of all that research entails but at the same time teaching them the ability to discern the quality and integrity of information based on the credibility of sources:

> The world is different. The two biggest things that impact me as a faculty member, my students, and the whole educational enterprise is information overload and stress. The paradox of choice. There is so much that we all have access to, and as a community of nutritionists, the internet is filled with people who are spouting nutrition and food information that is not based in science. But who's the expert anymore? Right? You can Google it, and that's the reality.

Continuing her story, she makes clear that the information overload is not unique to herself; it contributes to the level of stress and anxiety that students of all kinds exhibit, in particular those whose economic and educational experiences early in life may not have provided a full understanding of college study, its costs, and what lies beyond graduation:

> This whole information overload blends in perfectly with my diversity work. The stress on students today seems different. I can look back on my own experience as the first in my family to go to college, but I see more students down in my office hours with tears, with stress, with mental health issues, with financial burdens. "Am I even going to be able to get a job?" I know this isn't just happening on our campus, that it's a trend across the nation.

CHANGING CURRICULUM FOR A CHANGED WORLD

Not surprisingly, faculty use their disciplines as analogs for what is happening to themselves, their families, and their students. Many faculty members voice the awareness that changes in knowledge and its applications call for revisions of the curriculum and the skills they teach their students:

> The world has changed. We used to be an industrial society, and now we're a global economy, and I think our students are looking for instant gratification now. It's not the way for me to grade something. And the way

we teach? We teach differently. We now need to teach the ability to learn because you have to be a lifelong learner. You have to master the ability to critically think and problem-solve, so our curriculum has to change in order to incorporate those kinds of competencies in our courses. Before, I could teach CPR, which is really a skill. I mean, one, two, three, four, and five. But now you need to think critically about a given scenario: "What would you do in this scenario?" It's not enough for me to say it takes eight steps for me to do this.

Those in disciplines that train their students for a changing job market in many ways had the best seat at the table. Here is a lifelong teacher in an agricultural college coming increasingly to focus on climate change:

The whole face of agriculture and environmental science is changing so fast. A lot of the challenges around climate change have arisen within our college in the last few years. It wasn't really there as much seven years ago, at least more broadly across the college. I don't know. I think the curriculum needs to change faster than we would like to do it.

What sharpened this teacher's perceptions? A research assignment interviewing managers at firms interested in hiring graduates of the program:

There are changes in society and in climate and in the world that have bearing on what we teach. One thing that I heard from almost all of the people we interviewed, particularly in the larger firms, was, "Here's what we expect students coming out of college to know and here's what we're going to teach them because we're the only ones that can teach them. These are things that are changing fast and specific to the company. And we'll spend two years training somebody once we hire them. And so that's OK. We don't need you to do that." And then we'd spend a lot of time trying to figure out what's this and what's that.

The nature of the jobs is changing fast enough that we're not going to keep up with certain aspects of that at a university. I think the industry knows that. I wish I had asked somebody this, but my perception was that the amount of training that these firms do for their new employees has probably increased over the last several decades. They see a need to fill in the gaps that we can't meet and that gap is probably getting bigger. I didn't hear anybody say that our students aren't up to speed. They said that's fine. They said it was the professional skills that they felt were really lacking, so they were the big proponents of us doing more experiential learning so that students get more experience in the workplace. They wanted us big time to require a second language, because all of these employers hire people who have to work across a lot of cultural differences. I remember my son went and spent a couple of months in India, and when he came back, the thing that he said that struck me the most was, "Dad, I've never been so aware of the color of my skin." And I thought that's an experience that everybody ought to have.

Just as often, however, there is a pushback against the notion of training students. There are programs of study in many two- and four-year institutions that train students for specific careers. In other departments and institutions, though, the idea that the faculty's job is to prepare students for the labor market is just one more change lots of faculty don't like. Liberal arts faculty, in particular, keep looking for a different approach:

> What reproduces itself here is often this: "OK, how do we please our customers? How do we train them in some ways to be good customers? How do we send them out in the world to get a job?" That is a system that is so entrenched here, and if you really want change, you change that. That's my opinion. Now, it's also in some ways totally unrealistic to think that. But it feels to me as if what higher education could do, if people put their mind to it, is to pause this kind of sense of the student as a customer—not as a citizen—which I think is rampant now in higher education, and say, "No, that's not all you are. You may be that, but that's not all you are."

In part, as we have already observed, changing times mean changing pedagogies. Throughout the faculty stories we collected runs a curious nostalgia for the days of the big lecture, the big performance. Many faculty members were strongly influenced by mentors whose method was very much that of the sage on the stage. Some accounts attest to the power and impact that is possible through that style as something that their own students may never fully appreciate. At the same time, these faculty members can accept and even affirm the new realities of today's classrooms:

> There was one guy who taught a European history course my freshman year. He had been teaching there for forty years or something, and he had these set lectures that were beautifully crafted, and you were just supposed to sit there and take it all in. You were a spectator, and at the end of every lecture, he received applause, and then he walked out of the room to applause. So we've definitely changed quite a bit from that. I'd like more interaction in my classroom through interrogations of documents.

Roles and Rules for Different Times

Eventually, many of the faculty we met came to talk about their own lives and how and why they have changed. A recurrent theme is the sense of a growing generational divide in which different generations of faculty

members have different experiences. As in any era, those who enjoy the greatest discretion in how they fulfill their responsibilities are senior faculty. It is
not uncommon to find accounts of senior faculty members who are, in some
sense, exemplary citizens of the institution, demonstrating what it can mean
to change with the times:

> Regardless of how successful they've been previously, we see our senior-
> most faculty involved in some of our most innovative teaching projects.
> For instance, we run these "write your article in twelve weeks" writing
> groups. Of course, they are full of new faculty, but then one of the most
> senior faculty members in the College of Business is a regular participant.
> The summer workshops are filled with part-time faculty, who also hold
> employment outside of the university. There's also a gentleman who is a
> regular participant who is one of the most senior members of the political
> science faculty. He was one of my mentors when I was an undergraduate
> student. So there's definitely a generational shift going on here, just
> like everywhere else, and there are certainly faculty that are resistant to
> change on all levels. But even the most senior and respected members of
> our faculty recognize that this is not the same university that they entered
> thirty years ago.

Less heartening are accounts of how the experiences of faculty members
differ by generation. And then there is tenure and the stories about the process,
both the circumstances and the tensions that have become part and parcel of
the problem. Some stories from untenured faculty members recount themes
of conflicting signals from an institution—on the one hand, from administrators seeking to fill service posts in institutional governance, and on the other,
from faculty personnel committees that subject all tenure bids to the classic
criteria of research and publication.

An especially telling instance of that theme is of a now fully tenured communications professor who almost didn't achieve that mark:

> I came into a program that had all full-tenured faculty, and they had been
> tenured, full professors for a long time. I had a hard time going through
> the review for tenure and the promotion process. They didn't know a
> lot. The two new people that came in before me, one did not make it
> through the system, and the second one they brought in was much more
> mature and a one-person workhorse. It's the kind of hire every depart-
> ment wants. They're going to come in and kill themselves. So when I
> came along ABD [All but Dissertation], there wasn't good guidance on
> how important it was to finish. I hadn't finished the dissertation for two
> years. But I was never prompted. I mean, obviously, you want to, but it

seemed like, "Oh, there's all these important things they want you to do here."

So that put me in a hole that led to a tenuous process in the sixth year where the department supported it, tenure and promotion; the college level did not. The chair did not. Then I met with the union. And I had a lot of conversations. I knew going in it was problematic. I didn't have enough publications. I didn't receive any kind of negative ratings until the fifth year. And you know you just don't—you just don't know what you don't know.

So basically, it was a contentious process. But I also learned that at the college level, there was one person that led the charge to not go with the department, and that was our department representative. That person had a lot of sway. And it was difficult to understand how they could be so different than the department. So I kind of took it upon myself, and the union helped me to advocate, which all led to additional evidence going through additional advocacy meetings with the provost at the end of the case and arguing my case to the provost face-to-face.

A DOMINANT COMMITMENT TO RESEARCH

Research and publications are now more important to faculty promotion than ever, a changed circumstance that has sparked a renewed argument about what ought to be important at an institution committed to the teaching of undergraduates. It is a dispute that plays out differently across different disciplines and different institutions, with the sciences usually assumed to be the most hard-nosed in their support of research as a faculty member's first priority. However, we also heard from science faculty members who despair of advancing their careers, as budgets for scientific research stagnate and grant proposals face increasingly competitive odds. The proportion of successful grant proposals has fallen below 15 percent nationally, with the majority of successful applications granted to well-established senior investigators at major research universities. But the place of research and publication in faculty promotion is also an argument that can divide older and younger faculty within the sciences as well as within the humanities and the social sciences. Here is a veteran physicist at a major liberal arts college summing up what she believes:

> In order to maintain our standing, liberal arts colleges are becoming more and more like research institutions. That's something that has always concerned me. We have all of these young guns, who are incredibly talented researchers, and they want to be able to have the time to do their research and to pursue all these fantastic ideas. And that creates a tension, because it pulls the institution in a certain direction. I don't know how we're going

to manage that balance, but since I got here nineteen years ago, I have seen us gradually becoming more and more research oriented, even as we're still teacher-scholars. The scholarship part, however, really does take more and more of people's time without having the kind of support structure that we need, particularly in the sciences, to do all of that work effectively. I don't have a crystal ball for where that's going in the future, but I know that for our national prominence, it's very important. My guess is that's not going to change too much, but I hope we don't keep going too much in the direction of the research end of things.

The change humanists find easiest to lament is the triumph of the specialist. Count the number of times this professor of philosophy and religion does so:

I don't have statistics for it, but my impression is that within the last three or four years, we've had quite a lot of younger faculty come in due to retirements and not because of any problems. These younger faculty have varying degrees of experience in what a liberal arts education is. I would say there's a tendency for them to be more specialist trained, so it takes a conscious effort on the part of many of us to give them a larger sense of what liberal arts would look like. I think most of the pressures placed on the graduate students at most of our PhD-producing institutions are to specialize and to become really good at certain very limited things. They may have had a broader liberal arts foundation in their undergraduate education, but in the process of graduate education, that was not really a priority.

Regardless of rank, there is an insistence upon equality, and there's often an encouragement of junior faculty, even of untenured faculty, to take service positions. It's partly administrative decisions that contribute to this. When hires are made—for example, if junior faculty or recently tenured faculty are appointed to leadership hiring committees, say for a dean—then you have individuals who have not necessarily been in the institution very long, even though they may think they've been here for a while. We have a fairly vocal and empowered younger faculty, and if they're specialists, they don't necessarily understand areas outside of their studies. I noticed this most, I guess, in the sciences and in the behavioral sciences because that's where we've had a lot of hiring, and I don't think they know what philosophy and religion are. They maybe took a philosophy course somewhere, but they don't comprehend the dynamics of those disciplines and the purpose of those disciplines.

I'm a humanist, right? These are the things that I think I'm here to defend. I'm not opposed to the sciences, but at specialist institutions, the people that are coming from high-powered PhD programs need an education in the broader liberal arts, which has not necessarily been much of their graduate study. And if the hiring process isn't alerted to that, if the people that are hiring their junior colleagues in these disciplines are not attentive to that, then they can have a fairly superficial understanding of at least a third of the campus in humanities disciplines and their purpose. That's what we run into.

A PANORAMA OF MUSINGS

As we suggested at the outset of this chapter, faculty know about change, are prepared to talk about it, but mostly want to do so in subdued and tentative ways. In our travels across eleven quite different institutions, we encountered no faculty that we would call "shouters." There were no Jeremiahs or Cassandras, no sense of impending doom, no looming Armageddon. What struck us in the end was the extent to which our individual conversations, nearly forty of which explicitly focused on higher education's changing circumstances, expressed what we came to call "musings"—thoughts on subjects such as a changing emphasis in what is studied, in methods of teaching, and in the value of an education that includes engagement with different fields of knowledge. Among those conversations was an extended observation by a linguist, ten years into his career as a full-time scholar-teacher. It is a colloquy that easily doubles as a summary of the dilemmas and apprehensions many faculty bring with them to discussions of change:

> We've had a number of talks, whether it's by faculty here on campus or by visitors, about the future of liberal arts education and how we need to adjust. I'm pretty sure the faculty have different views on the issues, and some have very strong views about liberal arts education and what we do by providing opportunities for students to focus on intellectual growth and emphasizing abilities like critical thinking, problem solving, debating, writing. These are general guidelines that a lot of people use to approach their teaching.
>
> There is also the claim that change is needed in a liberal arts education, given the cost of education and changes in students' interests. A lot of students, for example, are now interested in more experiential learning, internships, things that they can put on their CVs, I guess. My worry is that we're going to move more and more away from a commitment to learning through traditional coursework. I'm open to innovations, but I don't want to just dump the whole system of lecturing and discussion to emphasize students doing internships with companies that I know nothing about. It's valuable experience, but is it learning in the sense of a liberal arts education?

There has been a decline in the humanities and languages and more interest in the sciences now. Natural science is a nice major for premed students who are interested in medical school. They'll typically go in that direction. I think that's fine, but would we conclude from that that we should move away from the humanities? And if we move away from languages, would we be moving away from cultural literacy? We talk a lot about diversity and inclusivity and cultural literacy, but is talking about them enough, or do we actually need to make a clear effort to expose learners during their college experience to different aspects of this vast, diverse world? If they are not learning foreign languages, how are they going to learn about these other cultures?

Some students are more practical in their way of thinking, and parents really pay a lot of money for their children's educations. Just think about the cost of this college. You don't want them to incur debt that they have to repay over many years. If I were to guess, I think the debate will be around the cost, about the feasibility of our curriculum, moving away from traditional teaching to some other forms of learning and providing less exposure for our students to cultural literacy and diversity.

Faculty Voice

NOPE, TOO BUSY

How does someone who is hired to be an associate dean to develop a new curriculum cope when all the faculty who worked on a major course revision don't have time to teach it? After three years of course redesign, this administrator / faculty member at a major research university just dove in and did it herself . . . with a little help from her friends and an unexpected new classroom. The result was a spectacularly successful team-taught, yearlong experience where both the students and the faculty learned from one another.

We admit into the College of Biological Sciences people that intend to major in biological sciences, and we don't trap them here. They can change their minds. In the past, there were three different paths of introductory biology that students could take. One was no intro college biology at all. You just "AP-tested out" of all of it. One was a one-semester kind of survey class, and the other was a two-semester survey class that was a mixture of something aimed more at nonmajors together with something that was more like what biological sciences majors would do. I looked at the data for the three tracks, and the data were really clear. Most of the students who took AP biology and tested out of intro biology dropped out of the college and left. The ones who took one semester were a little better, and the ones who took a full year were the ones who stayed. It was interesting because it was inverted. We'd built this system because we didn't want to slow down the students who had taken AP biology; we'd get them right into the upper-division courses. They didn't do well.

As a result of this failure, we got together a big team of faculty that spent two years talking about the curriculum and what should be in this one class for incoming students. It was decided it would be a yearlong class. An interesting kind of goal was trying to integrate the biological concepts of scales of time and space; that is, a typical kind of sequence would start with molecules and then build up from there until you got to ecosystems. Or start with ecosystems and drill down until you got to molecules. So everything was kind of chapter by chapter by chapter. What the group designed kept us going back and forth at different levels of scale so that students were wrestling with things at a small level and then going and seeing the related material at a larger level. After two years of making the framework of what this course would be, another group spent a year designing the actual course and coming up with a syllabus, et cetera.

I led those conversations and made sure we made the agendas and brought in external experts. At about the same time, I became involved in this National Academies Summer Institute group, which also was very helpful in laying out the education literature in a way that was really easily comprehensible. It took out a lot of the jargon.

Here's what happened. You know, I was brought here as an associate dean to help the college improve the curriculum. The people on the planning committee were very carefully chosen as people who were likely to want to teach this new class; we'd been talking for three years about it, and the time came for actually teaching the course. Everyone—every single person—said, "Nope, too busy." And frankly, I wasn't ready to wait, so I just lunged in, and using all of this team-based, active learning, I taught the first course.

The idea is it's not about the lecture; it's not about what you say; it's about what students do. The idea was to hold these students accountable and have very high expectations. Typically, it's a two-semester course, team-taught by different people who have slightly different areas of expertise, and it was just remarkable. We were able to watch students imagine things that don't yet exist. We were learners alongside the students; we were learners from the students.

This whole idea happened right at exactly the same time as another crazy coincidence. We were planning the summer before we launched this new sequence, "Foundations of Biology," to teach it in a lecture theater because there wasn't anything else here, but we got a call in maybe June from our Office of Classroom Management. They said, "We're interested in making 'scale-up-style' classes, which are roundtables in classrooms with white boards and technology, and we have this room down in the basement." When I went down there, I asked them something I've been asking them ever since. I said, "Can you make it bigger?" They were planning for like a 45-person classroom, but we ended up with an active learning classroom that held 135 people, and we launched the class there. Of course, the classroom supported so much of what we were trying to do that it just ended up being really successful.

It was just a pilot class because they were planning this new building and they wanted to see how these rooms worked. They were going to study how the faculty interacted and the students . . . and we were ready to go. Oh, my gosh, it was like a gift from . . . yeah, it was like providential. The thing that's great about that classroom is that once you're on the same level, you're not apart from the students. You're with the students. You can go and sit down at the table, and you can kind of probe what their understanding is. You start to get a real deep respect for what they're capable of. I was surprised before, when I discovered you didn't need a lot of biology content knowledge to have good thoughts, but this classroom and approach was icing on the cake.

At the beginning the sandbox was small. It was a little more structured. I taught with a colleague who felt that the students should be able to choose their own topic. I thought, "OK, let's give it a try." Here was the project we had them work on: identify a problem of social value that your group cares about and figure out a way to use genes and gene technology with an evolutionary perspective to solve it. Holy cow, all the projects were good. Some were pretty predictable, but some were so off-the-scale creative. If we hadn't asked them to choose their own, we wouldn't have known that they're capable of amazing things.

The very first time we did that, one group had a veteran who was coming back to college, and he helped convince his team to work on camouflage clothing. The group's idea was to make a kind of clothing that would work like the skin of a squid, and they would use bacteria of different colors. They could then have some electrical impulses in this clothing, and it could sense the surrounding area and change colors. It sounds really science fiction-y. The first step toward the project had to be viable science that could be done now, but the big idea didn't necessarily have to be able to be done now. And of course the army and other people are working on similar kinds of things like this camouflage.

I remember so clearly; I can say, "It's that table over in that corner." I walked over there, and the very first day after they were discussing what problems they were going to use, I walked over and listened to a discussion of creating unicorns. I thought, "Oh, this is not what we had in mind." And then sure enough, they self-corrected until they came up with this really interesting idea about limb regeneration. They looked at the literature, and they found that there's a certain kind of collagen that gets turned on in a certain kind of chemical, and they were going to try that. People had used it for regenerating the tips of fingers in humans. So they were going to mass-produce this chemical using genetic engineering and things. Anyway, it's all good. It's all good.

I've learned over and over and over again that you have to trust the students. You give them space, you trust them, you give them feedback, and they just will amaze you. I think that that's the sad thing when I go into a classroom and it's this lecture about stuff that they can read about. It's not tapping their creativity. In that kind of environment, they have no possibility of seeing themselves as scientists or how scientists would approach this or stuff they already know. So what do we not know? What would be an important problem? Can you use this photosynthesis process to create artificial solar panels to produce energy? I don't know what it would be, but it really saddens me that those situations are not allowing them to flourish. They're not allowing them to practice not just critical thinking but creative thinking.

Open-ended problem solving and that group process—I've come to really rely on that. We did learn early on that students, just like many of my colleagues, are not very good at working in teams. I'm not always good at working in teams either, but helping them learn strategies for how to be successful, how to feel comfortable giving honest feedback in a kind way that's going to help the others improve—I think that that's probably been the theme. I keep redefining my job. It's not my job to teach them writing; it's not my job to teach them teamwork, but I'm realizing that really when all is said and done, that skill is going to be way more important to them than remembering any of the biology, because they can always go look that up, particularly now. The other revolution that we are wrestling with is how to design and develop learning experiences in the world we now live in, where instant access to all of human knowledge is available to us.

CHAPTER 5

Losses and the Calculus
of Subtraction

NO AMOUNT OF EXHORTATION can disguise what nearly every faculty member intrinsically understands: doing with less is no one's nirvana. The instinct everywhere is to resist those forces that threaten to diminish or subtract what the community believes to be valuable and hence inviolate. Among the toughest moments in a faculty member's professional life are those in which a once admired department is about to be dismantled. And it is just as likely that such reductions in the name of consolidation will be more than matched by additions somewhere else. The German department disappears, and communication emerges as a newly dominant major.

Some of the most dispiriting tales we collected were stories of decline and loss. While changes in the general knowledge base are at times responsible, the dominant force for contraction was a pronounced shift in student interests. And what the market dictated was often reinforced by the need to rebalance the budget, wrapped in public calls for more accountability and efficiency.

The results can devastate whole departments as well as individual faculty members. The prospect of losing all that one has worked to build and improve through the course of a career produces emotions ranging from guilt and shame to anger. Across the campuses we visited, veteran administrators told us how they had weathered the dramas surrounding the closure of a department while at the same time acknowledging that such closures almost always diminished faculty morale. In candid talks with us, some institutional leaders wondered whether the revenue savings from a department closure warranted the years of rancor that so often followed.

Almost always, the faculty response to the prospect of reducing or closing a program is one of resistance. Faculty members who may be divided on some issues will band together in defense of a program threatened with reduction or elimination. It is often perceived as a case of "There but for the grace of God go I." The pushback against subtraction almost always produces stratagems designed to thwart each and every plan that promises fewer course offerings or faculty reassignments or that transfers a vacant faculty position from one department to another. Occasionally an administration will persist, achieving the necessary reduction through protracted and often painful negotiations that put off the foreboding outcome at least for the present. Negotiation can also yield a result that allows both a department and an administration to achieve their most important interests. The more likely result, however, is no result at all, as the administration comes to conclude that the hoped-for savings and consolidations are simply not worth the price it is being asked to pay.

CURRICULUM CONSTRAINTS

Almost no one emerges from these situations either energized or reassured. The stories that faculty members as well as administrators told of working to counter the omen of subtraction are almost uniformly gloomy, though the saddest tales came from humanities departments in liberal arts colleges facing diminished enrollment. Some of these colleges have sought to enhance the size of their student bodies by creating new programs with a more practical emphasis and proven market appeal, leading one foreign language faculty member to observe,

> Because of the public's desire to have young people graduate with skills that are immediately employable, we've struggled like other small liberal arts colleges to protect our values and our mission of providing a broad education. There has been some tension between providing both skills and a broad education. As we try and survive and make sure that we are "sustainable" in the next century, the college has moved very, very strongly into creating programs that probably are not traditionally in the liberal arts, such as the new nursing program.
>
> On the one hand, the idea was that these programs were going to bring in students, period. But those students would also enroll in the arts and humanities, in the social sciences, in those areas that we think are viable and important so that students become citizens, not just wage earners. We were hoping that those students would become more community oriented by virtue of coming to the college, and the numbers, of course, would help.
>
> But what we're finding, at least in arts and humanities, is that these programs, especially like the nursing program, have so many required courses, so many credits that the students must earn, that they finally are very, very limited in what they can take. And I have noticed this in particular in the language courses because I have a lot of students who say that they would like to go on, and in fact they see the value of studying more language. They have no time; they have no time. And so it's a great idea that we have

moved in these directions, partly because we believe that nurses who are working with the public need to be broadly educated. But on the other hand, they are very limited in what they can take. They have very little flexibility in the program. So it's almost counterproductive.

If the strategy of adding a new program to help all boats rise in the college has not exactly worked as expected, it is not just small language departments that suffer. It is the ideal of liberal arts education itself, which affirms the value of introducing students to a range of knowledge, and of instilling skills of independent thought and expression that prepare graduates for life as well as work.

In other instances, faculty in threatened departments talked about the expanding requirements mandated by departments with strong, fully enrolled majors constraining their students' ability to take courses of interest that do not relate directly to their major field. Reflecting on the demands placed on science majors, a professor of psychology, often thought of as a kindred discipline, gave expression to the constraint of choice that many students experience:

> I think it's hard in some particular disciplines to streamline the curriculum, especially if you think about premedicine. They have to take the prerequisite classes. They have to take classes that are going to prepare them for the MCAT, which is the large test they need to take in order to gain admission to medical school. I think there are important courses outside of the discipline too, in the arts, humanities, and social sciences for those students. In general, I think our students do take way more than the 136 credits that are required of them, but I think a lot of that is that many of them start in a given area and then they decide to change, and so they have to add those particular credits. I think the overall curriculum needs to be analyzed, but like I said, in the sciences especially, I think it's difficult to streamline.

STRATEGIES

The sense of austerity surrounding an institution or a department sometimes yields strategies to avert what could otherwise accelerate a downward trend. The gambit of creating a new program that prepares students for more practical and immediate career options is one that many smaller liberal arts colleges have tried with varying success. Sometimes an individual department can produce a win through a fortuitous circumstance that solves a problem in a way that none might have foreseen. A professor of modern languages at a small college explained,

We had a professor who was nearing retirement. The languages department has this rotating chair, and I was chair too at the time he retired. I wrote as part of the long-term plan a proposal for a Global Studies program as well as to keep German and add Chinese. I had to argue why it was important to keep German, and I researched other schools, what their language offerings were. This was probably ten years ago or more now, and a reasonable number of schools in the state still did offer German. We also have a lot of people living in the region for whom Germany was their home country, and so there are those cultural links. I was able to argue that we should keep German. So we replaced the retirement with my younger colleague who is professor of German. She also then got the Chinese program going. So they got two things for their one, if you will. I think that was also part of what allowed us to keep German.

I'm worried that my colleagues won't be able to make the same pitch for French when I'm gone. I hope they can.

Elsewhere it was a psychology department that, confronted with the necessity of reducing the number of course offerings in its roster, took the step of moving the content of some courses into other courses its majors must take:

Ninety percent of the time, we don't cut courses when we add. The other 10 percent is when our registrar has in the last few years gone through and said, "Hey, we haven't offered this course in X number of semesters. Are we going to keep it, or do we need to get rid of it?" And so we've done some culling. An example from psychology is cognitive psychology, and I've taught that here. It's a staple in psych departments, but we decided here to take it off the books; we haven't taught it now for three years. What we decided to do was to take that information in cognitive psychology and work it into other courses so we can give exposure to cognitive psychology in a neuroscience course; it's in a social psychology course; it's in a developmental psych course; it's in an experimental psych course. While it'll look different for our students not to have a cognitive psychology class on their transcripts, as long as we can communicate to the outside world that we took this material and put it in these other areas, then we're OK.

The risk in this case is that the transcripts of psychology majors from the institution may appear deficient to a graduate program or employer looking particularly for a course enrollment in the subject. From the standpoint of the department's faculty, however, the step taken would seem to have achieved the goal of reducing total course offerings without sacrificing essential content.

BEYOND DISPLACEMENT—TOWARD RENEWAL

Other tales came from those who had a leadership role in creating a sense of renewed identity and purpose for faculty members whose home department had been recombined into a larger, composite academic unit. The feeling of having lost one's original academic and cultural bearings is tough to bear, making it a considerable challenge to help a newly combined unit find common purpose.

One account from a faculty member who had come into a leadership role with no previous administrative experience reflected the learning curve that begins with a realization that data are not the only factors in determining the fate of shrinking departments:

> Our school had a set of majors that were probably put together fifty years ago, and during that period of time, a lot of change had taken place. We tried to make this data driven as much as possible, so it wasn't "Oh, this is a good idea," but we looked at the change in the demographics of the students and interests of our students over the last thirty years.
>
> I mean, it had completely shifted. We went from like 10 percent women to 66 percent women, you know, all of those types of changes. Mostly suburban and urban compared to thirty years ago, when we were mostly rural. So it was a very big change, change in interest, and it was pretty clear that some of the majors we had really just weren't what they had been; I mean, there's nobody in them.
>
> So we sort of thought, "Well, that's a no-brainer. There are three here that we just need to get rid of." We made that suggestion, and the pushback was absolutely amazing—the reasoning that groups of faculty came up with for trying to keep a major that had one student per year, and we had to listen to those and had to be very attentive. It became pretty clear, OK, that we needed to back up and do this in a much more comprehensive manner.

The stories of helping displaced faculty members find a new departmental home reflect an essential first step: the need to commence a process for defining a coherent purpose that encompasses the skills of all faculty members within the newly constituted department. One story told of a department that needed to redefine its mission and vision as the market for its offerings had migrated to other institutions:

> The department was in effect something of the legacy from what had been vocational-technical education fifty years ago. And vocational-technical education, which is vitally important to life in the twenty-first century in America, is not an active area of academic research by any faculty at

this entire university. What had happened over a number of years was the people pursuing those certifications did them at the next tier of public institutions in the state, and their tuition structure is such that it was less expensive for the practitioners to complete their certifications.

As a result, the enrollment here dwindled and dwindled and dwindled. Meanwhile, the enrollment in this human resource development department and other specialized adult education was growing, so those ultimately became the focus. Those people in that old vocational-education program felt like their department had been shut down and that they had been crammed into leftover space in this department.

So there was some resentment. Well, the individual who was chair at that time wasn't mean spirited about it. He just wasn't particularly insightful about what I would describe as the organizational development needs of the separate groups coming together.

Succession event: new department chair, and that's when the dean approached me about being associate chair. This new chair is a very thoughtful, extremely smart woman, who is very sensitive to the organization development needs but had no clue what to do about it, so I had a receptive ear and could say, "Well, let me share with you what an organization might do to help." And initially I needed a lot of help and direct feedback. Though I earned my degrees at this institution, I had worked for some time in the business sector, and I was often told, "We just don't do things that way here in academia." Now seven years, eight years later, I don't; I rarely run into that, but the first year or two, I had those things back at me. Every week I'd have one or two of those things back at me.

But between the dean's interest and commitment to being fair and inclusive and thoughtful and being a great listener and also being very direct in pushing back and saying here's what would work and won't work in an academic environment, it was a great learning experience for me, and I in turn could help her to guide the entire faculty through a series of activities that helped us to clarify what our shared purpose is and what our mission is here at this university, and by the way, it is to be resoundingly great in our program track.

If you're at an R1 institution and you aren't thinking that way, get out of the way. You know what I'm saying? So what's going to distinguish you? What contributions are your faculty making that are world-beating sorts of contributions? And how can we collaborate in a way that makes this a supportive and friendly environment or base of operations and explore what is the core that would run through the graduate learning experience for all of our grad students? The former chair guided the faculty through that process over a series of years answering those kinds of questions.

It was focusing on what is our reason for being, what's our mission and our purpose, and how do we do it in a way that's supportive and collaborative? The result of this process is that our department really does feel supportive and collaborative. And people who've come to us from other departments have said, "Wow, what a great academic environment you've got in this department." Well, that didn't happen by accident.

That focus insistently over three or four years is what it took to really get the faculty to lean in around here and be supportive—tough but very supportive of each other. A lesson from this work is that organizational change takes time and is messy.

The successes chronicled in this story provide an example of how an organizational change could help a unit survive, due in large part to the care that was taken in creating a new programmatic identity based on what the faculty themselves wanted from the larger configuration. Another lesson from this story is the importance of sustaining that departmental conversation about purpose as new circumstances evolve and as changes in enrollment, funding, or leadership create new challenges.

MIGRATION OF LEARNING CENTEREDNESS

A similar story about helping a group of faculty members move from a feeling of loss to one of renewed purpose occurred in another newly combined department. In this case, the person who took on a key role in fostering a sense of collective identity stressed the importance of students and their learning as core to the departmental culture:

> I would want to impart to somebody else trying to do curricular changes to really figure out what are some of the core values that drive the group that's endeavoring to make the change or initiate the new thing. I think innovation without an explicit, identified, articulated core is easy to get lost in the process. At a university this big with so many stakeholders, there are a lot of parts to changing something or initiating something. And I think if you don't have that very simple core to go back to over and over, you can get lost—when you're talking with deans or talking with students or prospective students or faculty or you're talking with the layers of approval, the money piece. So you have to keep, I think, a simple core.
>
> Building that core looked different over the decade that we've been doing it, but I would say in the beginning what it looked like was really acknowledging a need to create something because we were a new department. We resulted from a previous structural reorganization of three colleges.
>
> I think what I observed is that if change is seen as a zero-sum game, it's not change. You know, there's kind of a sentiment that says, "Well, you

can add something or you can do something, but not if it's going to affect what I do or my grad students or my course or my enrollments."

As a young faculty member, I found that very frustrating because what was at the center of that was the faculty members and their understanding of their area, right? And their importance rather than the students. So when we got started in this new department, one of the things that we really tried to emphasize was that students are always at the center of this. What do we want the students to do? What do we want them to know? What do we want them to bring? What do we want them to discover? Always really trying to bring it back to the students. It wasn't a zero-sum game, but it was a zero-base.

For all the sustained work through the course of a decade, however, the innovation that had come to embody this combined department came to an abrupt end. The decisive factor in this case was a financial shortfall, leading to a change in leadership that, in turn, brought different priorities and recastings:

> That's right, our program went up, and it launched, and it was very effective, and within a few years, the overall department was in financial disarray and was put into receivership for a year, and then they hired an outside chair who was not the right fit, I would say, at all. Had the right pedigree and looked very impressive. I was on the search committee. Not the right person for the job. And within two years, all of us who had been hired, three people who had been hired for this new program had left. The program was gone. Other programs were gone, and the chair was gone within two years. It's interesting to me to think too about how long it took him to get it, and it really was a dynamic and exciting place. But it couldn't survive. Because someone coming in thinks, "Well what's this? I want to put the resources into theory and the thing that I know and . . . And I want these kind of people here."

From the story of the dissolution of the program the group had built, this faculty member went on to reflect about the intensified competition for resources—in state legislatures, in higher education, and in the home institution itself. Ultimately, it was financial distress resulting from the loss of students that led to the unhinging of the curriculum this group had developed. Not least among the casualties of revenue competition, by this person's account, was the sense of value accorded to effective teaching and student learning in the institution:

> Well, I don't think most of these changes would be just specific to my group, but certainly we are in a state institution. It is governed by the legislature to some extent and the board of regents. I think when I started

here, we got, maybe it was twenty-eight cents on the dollar from state funds, and now it's like twelve cents. And yet our costs are going up, right? Insurance, infrastructure, everything is more expensive even if you're being conservative on how you spend, just having people is more expensive. So certainly there isn't enough money where there used to be, and the question is, how do you get more money? How do you remain profitable even in a nonprofit? So you're just sustainable? And locally, in this institution, part of where that has played out is in competition for students.

We have a budget model in which dollars follow butts-in-seats. And I think that was implemented just before I came to the university, and as you know, they started that model at a time when belts weren't tight. But as belts have gotten tighter, it becomes a dogfight for students. And it has nothing to do with what's good for students. It has nothing to do with—to me—what it should have to do with, and I think it could be changed. Students are fluid. They move around a university, and my belief, my very strong belief, is that it's good for students to have a well-rounded education.

I think it's great for them to take all kinds of classes. Even if they know what they're going to do before they come here, it's great for them to have that exposure to different ways of thinking, different ways of creating knowledge, different ways of doing research, different ways of communication, different ways of saving the world.

I think that's less and less possible if they are more and more contained to a unit so that that unit can generate all the tuition possible from that student. So I would say all these layers of financial change are certainly big. This university for me, and I would say for people in my unit and actually in my college too is increasingly a revenue-focused university. It's been implicit for a while, but it's getting more and more explicit.

For me, where the student is, I think, that's almost as lost as where the teacher is. I study teaching. My pedagogy is my area of interest, and I just think that, even with the academic technology, there's more talk about things that are teaching and learning related. But I don't see more infrastructure or commitment to training teaching in faculty and future faculty. I guess now I've been doing this twenty-five years, and it's shifted. I think of our center for teaching and learning, which used to be right in the center of campus, and it's literally been moved and moved. And it's way far away now. It's not near any buildings where teachers are. It's in the shadow of the new stadium.

This professor's reflections encompass what other faculty in a variety of settings have said about how their institutions were adrift, often usurped by programs of focused knowledge in the major and career preparation at the expense of learning that prepares graduates to understand themselves within larger traditions of knowledge. In the intensified competition for students and for dollars, what often falls to the wayside is a genuine concern for the learning that students experience through the curriculum and associated programs of education. The challenge to institutions of all kinds is to ensure the continued vitality of learning itself in a time of reduction and subtraction.

HOPEFUL PROSPECTS

In both of these tales of departments caught in a contracting vortex, the sense of a unifying purpose came about slowly. Progress was the result of tough-minded but respectful dialogue among faculty members brought together in search of common ground. The exchange of views, critiques, and responses and the exploration of possible arrangements that could prove satisfactory all characterize the process of negotiation, and in fact, the exchanges within these two departments exemplified negotiation extending through several years.

Some of the faculty we met told us of the importance of negotiation as a useful skill for faculty members in departments confronted with the possibility of reduction or closure, particularly if the parties in discussion commit to what the standard literature on the topic calls principled negotiation. As opposed to positional bargaining, successful negotiation can help a department and enable it to retain some things that it values most. Principled negotiation, as described by Roger Fisher and William Ury in *Getting to Yes: Negotiating Agreement Without Giving In* (1981), seeks to abide by several tenets: it seeks an agreement that can satisfy both parties, it proceeds beyond positions to explore the underlying *interests* that inform each party's stance, it seeks agreement based on common values, and it considers the quality as well as the substance of an agreement.

A professor with experience in this process describes what he terms "interest-based negotiation" as a useful process in the academy:

> IBN, interest-based negotiation. This was phenomenal. I came onto the team in the first year that IBN was implemented. The former negotiation method, "positional bargaining," is where the parties come to the table and say, "Here's our list of demands," and then you beat each other up and maybe you find some room to agree on something. For the most part, it's not very productive because you bring forward the solutions without ever talking about what the problems are. With interest-based negotiation, you say, "All right, what's the problem? Let's see if we can agree on what the problem is. And then let's identify our interests. So what are the interests of the various parties? Can we generate options to address the problem

that are consistent with the interests of the parties?" It's a very collaborative, very positive experience. That doesn't mean that it's not difficult and that there's not conflict, but you're starting from a place of consensus on what the problem is, and then you're trying to find solutions that address all interests.

One account of successful negotiation involved the Business department of that person's institution and the administration. In this case, the department held certain advantages; it was not in receivership and had no shortage of enrollments. The spirit of productive exchange through time yielded an agreement that in effect expanded the size of the pie by considering other arrangements that allowed both parties to achieve their interests:

Administration wanted to see a mandatory internship for all of our students in the business program that in theory was good but in reality was probably not going to work, so that took many, many meetings of conversations, discussions. I probably oversee more internships than anybody on this campus, but the problem is that we graduate sixty to eighty students a year and there are not sixty to eighty internships in this small town in the middle of nowhere. We didn't have sites, but we are connected to the Philadelphia Center and the Chicago Center for Interns. Unfortunately, the administration stated that our financial aid would not go with the student when they went off to Philadelphia or Chicago, so that reduced the number of opportunities there. What we came up with was a compromise. Yes, the students could do internships, but they could also do an applications course, they could do an independent study, they could do a thesis, and these options now give our faculty and students much more flexibility. So in the end, it was a nice compromise; it did work, but it took a while. Yeah, we went into it kicking and screaming, literally. It was, from our perspective as the business faculty, extremely worthwhile. I don't know if the administration would say the same thing because a lot of what they originally wanted us to do, we did not do. We now have specific majors in all the business fields we did not have before; we have a lot of flexibility in terms of applications for our students, and we got programs that were more than the thirty-six-hour requirement. The business faculty were kind of doing cartwheels down the hallway once it was finally approved. We like what we got.

THE PROBLEM WITH ADDITION

The Business department in that vignette achieved much of what it wanted, even though it did not get the ability to offer internships in programs that would require the transfer of institutional financial aid to external programs. The tenor of the story makes clear that the department's tactic was not one of positional bargaining, seeking a favorable outcome at any cost. Rather it was to engage the problem through principled negotiation, looking beyond initial positions to find favorable outcomes that could satisfy the interests of both parties and preserve the environment of collegiality and goodwill.

The Business department could negotiate from a position of comparative strength with its administration. There were no signs in this case of an academic unit facing declining enrollments and dimming prospects. But not every department enjoys that kind of bargaining advantage. Academic units facing the need to subtract and reduce often find that they have little to offer in return for sustaining support from an administration. No amount of wishing can restore student enrollments to their former levels; at best, a department might argue the need for the institution to mount an aggressive admissions effort to attract more students with an interest in the field.

Paradoxically, in many cases, the action taken to stave off subtraction is to add—new courses, new programs of emphasis within the major—or to continue to offer credit-bearing options to serve the needs of the major without taking away other parts of the curriculum that faculty members value. In more than a few cases, sustaining these options amounts to an add-on to a faculty member's standard responsibilities. Taking an overload for the indefinite future is the last act of resistance against the nemesis of reduction:

> I'm almost always in overload mode. Yes, this semester, for example, I am teaching four full-time courses, and then I have two independent studies on top of that. The normal course load would be three courses. And then I'm chairing the department, and that is an overload. The overloads come largely because you've got one- or two-person departments. I mean, I am essentially responsible for the French program. If I have a student or two students who need another course, and they've already had the course that I'm offering, I have no choice but to offer them another course as an independent study or something. You see, that's where the real issue comes in: we have to meet the needs of the students, and I have no colleague and no extra course to provide them unless I just do it out of my own hide.

In other cases, the act of addition results from a different though related phenomenon. In the following tale, a department that had grown substantially in enrollments without a concomitant increase in the number of faculty recognized that what had been constrained was the faculty's ability to serve students' learning needs:

There's information overload for all of us, and then the time scarcity. I have less one-on-one time with students now to really get to know them and what their unique needs are, and they don't get as much air time within the classroom. The Community Nutrition course I'm teaching this spring is a senior-level course with forty students. When I started teaching the same course here sixteen years ago, it was twelve to fourteen students. And when I got here sixteen years ago, food and nutrition sciences had about seventy-five majors. Now we have about three hundred, so it's definitely been a major that's grown in popularity. Several people were hired after I was hired in 2000, but then several retired, so we're about the same as when I came. But we have three hundred majors instead of seventy-five. We're not unique on the campus and not so unique in the country.

The problem with addition, then, takes two forms: it is the individual professor who teaches continually beyond the standard course and service assignments to sustain a viable major, and it is the faculty member who has experienced a several-fold increase in the number of majors for whom he or she is responsible. In both cases, the steady accretion of responsibilities yields a net decrease in the time and energy that anyone can devote to the tasks at hand. The portions grow smaller as the pie is cut into more servings. The inevitable result, as calibrated by the sheer metrics of human energy, is a decline in quality. Some parts of the individual or department agenda may continue to be fulfilled as effectively as ever, as judged by the most discerning standards. But in the array of tasks confronting any one person or organizational unit, those carried through at the highest standards of quality will be the ones that are valued most highly, while others receive uneven and more perfunctory attention.

The solution to the dilemma is certainly not to constrain the penchant for addition. What draws people to an academic career is nearly always the excitement of expanding one's horizons, discovering and pursuing new interests, and continuing a trajectory of intellectual and professional growth. Faculty members are inherently prone to create new things—new courses or programs that represent promising avenues for teaching or research. Yet without some commensurate reduction of existing responsibility, addition, in itself, becomes the face of subtraction. The limits of human energy ultimately confirm that continued addition is a zero-sum undertaking. Adding further tasks to a full workload is the individual version of the tragedy of the commons, overtaxing a finite resource beyond its capacity to sustain the whole.

Not surprising then, the prevailing instinct is to resist subtraction in all its forms at every turn. There is as well an impulse to avoid the reductions that subtraction brings through an act of addition, which paradoxically dilutes the feeling of achievement and satisfaction from the work taken on. The result of the push-pull of subtraction and addition is both a weariness and a cynicism that declares, up front, that there are no winners in any process of reform. A brief observation from a professor of long standing epitomized this dilemma, making clear that subtraction and addition are two sides of the same coin:

> People have certain investments in their little territories that they don't want to give up because we're all kind of independent contractors. We're very good at taking on something new that we want, but we're very bad at giving up something that we're comfortable with and we like. When we get everything that we want and we didn't give up anything that we didn't, then we're overworked, and we find a way to complain about that too.

Faculty Voice

Look, It's a Course . . . It's a Major . . . No, It's SUPERMAJOR!

This professor of modern languages has taught at the same liberal arts institution since 1996. Due to enrollment pressures, her college developed several signature programs that require more than thirty-six credits and typically have courses that must be taken sequentially. She and her faculty colleagues have dubbed these "supermajors" because of their requirements and intensity.

Maybe four or five years ago, there was a big push for signature programs. As much as we'd like to think we're a liberal arts institution, business and education have always been our bread and butter, our two cash cows, and then pre-med has always been one of the feathers in our cap. We have good results there.

We've had this expansion of the natural sciences to grapple with the kids who have been on the fringe of premed. They're maybe not going to make medical school, but they could get into occupational therapy or physical therapy. Or we could combine medicine and business for health care administration—all these sort of things. Great, that's fine. But instead of saying, "If you have a solid background in biology and a solid background in business, you could go forth and present yourself for a job in health care administration. We have created a new program in health care administration, which we call a 'supermajor.'" It used to be that all majors were thirty-six credits, but now we have majors out there that are bumping against fifty credits. I think that health care administration might be forty-eight, as well as biotechnology. There are a variety of programs like this. There are some others that get around this situation by talking about "the base major of thirty-six credits, and then there are these three tracks." The student ends up having to take twelve credits out of something else they had planned to take, and their programs have highly sequenced courses.

My department of modern languages is battling a number of the issues created by these supermajors. My colleague in French had three advanced-level French students who had already made it through the grueling, horrible part of learning French and were finally getting to the interesting stuff. They would have liked to continue, but because their first major (and we are always the second major) is one of these supermajors that requires an inordinate number of credits and is highly sequential, these students have a conflict of time, and they're going to pick their supermajor. And we're going to flow out of the pipeline.

Again, in the unintended consequences category is the first-year seminar, which has lots of good reasons for existing. If one of a student's four classes is the first-year seminar and one of their four classes is either their basic composition or their math proficiency, and they want to be in a supermajor track like premed, education, or business, they have to take at least one class in that track in order to stay on time toward graduation. They don't have any time for that liberal arts exploration or other requirements. For example, all of our students have to take at least one language course, so all of our 111 "first-year language courses" are full of juniors and seniors because they haven't had time before then to get that course into their schedule. Even if they decide, "Well, this was kind of fun," it's too late for them to take any more courses in a language.

There are too many draws on a limited resource of student time and faculty time, and there's very little coordination in terms of . . . oh, somebody somewhere needs to look at the master plan and say, "Just because you like to teach this class on Tuesday and Thursday at one o'clock, doesn't mean you get to, because this class and this class are constantly colliding." The students get caught in the middle and lose out. Yeah, so we do weird things, like we will put our upper-level classes on the schedule as "to be assigned" and then tell our students to enroll in our course after their schedules are fixed, and we'll then find a time for our course to meet. We stole this idea from the physics department that does this too. That's how we have to position ourselves to be able to protect our students, because if we said, "No, I'm going to teach it at this time and only at this time," then we wouldn't have half of our students. We'd not only be conflicting with the supermajors but with everyone else as well. We can only do this for the advanced students in our pipeline, and who knows how many we're losing at the lower levels? Who's in what class? Who needs which of our upper-level classes? What are they likely to need in their other major, and when are these courses offered? We ask all of these questions so that we don't cause undue conflicts. It's nuts.

So we say, "Oh, liberal arts, liberal arts," but there are so many widgets in the machine that work against that being able to happen. The bulk of students tend to be enrolled in these supermajors, which besides premed, business, education, and health care administration are integrated physiology and health science, nursing. Oh, good Lord! And new media studies is another one of the signature programs that came out, which has been a tremendously popular program, although it is less sequential, less rigid than having to get through

Communications 1 through 4 but is still a supermajor with a number of courses that have to be taken.

How did the signature programs—the supermajors—come about? Six or eight were probably proposed by groups of faculty, and maybe two were funded: nursing and new media. We proposed a signature program that would change a traditional modern languages in literature major into more of a global studies program. Political science also proposed something that was more global and would have linked up well with us. But we weren't sexy enough for this, and the administration was right. What's our draw? I can't in good faith say, "If we put this program together, boy, you are going to have more Spanish majors than you know what to do with." We don't go out and recruit Spanish majors. We go out and recruit people who want to be whatever they want to be *and* speak Spanish. We accommodate what they perceive to be their real professional goal.

There are now so many other programs that are in the supermajor track that we are more often than not a service to them. And there are lots of institutional structures that not only keep us there but force us more and more into that role.

I don't know. It's just a very dysfunctional way of looking at ourselves, and there are people who are convinced that having these supermajors and more research and publishing is how we are going to improve our ranking. Maybe there are a handful of parents somewhere out there doing their due diligence and checking up on what our endowment is or something else. But I don't think that's really what is going to sell this place to a lot of first- and second-generation kids. That's our audience.

The students of generations ago had a liberal arts education because they didn't have to worry about going out and making a living. They came from wealthy backgrounds, and it was a privilege to have the time to be able to think about the liberal arts. We then provided this education to a different segment of the population, and rightly so. It should not be only for the privileged few, but this was an easier sell when the economy was strong. I was a first-generation kid. My parents were convinced that it didn't matter what I studied, because I was going to be better off than they were just because I had gone to college.

PART FOUR

 Frustrations

CHAPTER 6

The Cost Conundrum

THUS FAR, WE HAVE focused on what faculty talk often and easily about—the importance of teaching, their quest for independence, and the elements of an academic life that keep them in the classroom. Just as important, however, are the topics faculty have difficulty discussing and often simply don't. The most obvious lacunae involved their institution's finances and the roles that what and how they teach play in making their institutions ever more costly.

THE TYRANNY OF UNFORESEEN CONSEQUENCES

We begin our exploration of what we came to call the "cost conundrum" with a story of an advanced graduate student interested in curricular reform. When Reyes Gonzalez began his doctoral training in 2013, he was already an accomplished professional—a tough-minded, inquisitive, no-nonsense CFO at a Catholic women's college in Milwaukee. But he was also a reformer, and in the Penn program in higher education management, he was attracted to the readings that emphasized the need for change in general and curricular change in particular. He absorbed the lessons Derek Bok taught in *Our Underperforming Colleges*, and while he was at it, imbibed a double dose of Zemsky, including *Checklist for Change*. At the end of his first year, he decided to write a dissertation that explored the connection between financial and curricular efficiency.

The resulting study focused on the processes and procedures employed by two faculty-driven reform efforts, one at a public comprehensive university and the other at a private midmarket liberal arts college. Both reform efforts achieved the educational goals the leaders had promised, but each subsequently proved problematic for the institution as a whole. In one, the revised curriculum required a substantial increase in the size of the faculty—an increase that, as it turned out, the institution could not afford. At the second institution, the reform contributed to a downturn in enrollments, which that institution could not afford either.

As Reyes reported, faculty-generated innovations abounded—the problem was that they were fraught with unintended consequences that in the end made them hopelessly expensive. Reyes's study more than reinforced the conclusions focusing on the disconnected nature of most curricula that we had drawn from our previous analyses of transcripts at two liberal arts colleges and two public comprehensive universities. The question we keep asking is, "Why?" And the answer we have come to is that neither the faculty nor the administration at most institutions really know what their education programs cost or the costs that must inevitably accompany nearly every effort to change how and what an institution teaches.

Too many faculty not only are unprepared but, in fact, are too often reluctant to talk about the costs and financial constraints that impact how they lead their academic lives. We were struck by how seldom the conversations we recorded talked about money or the role money played in the reform process. And often those who did talk about financial constraints were from disciplinary clusters experiencing shortfalls in either general enrollments or their major or, as was most often the case, both.

The elements of what we have come to call the cost conundrum reveal themselves in a variety of ways. There are departments or whole institutions that hover near the point of unsustainability, and their faculty express the anxiety this awareness creates, sometimes yielding actions to sustain enrollment that do not sit well from the standpoint of fidelity to the discipline or to students' learning needs. Another manifestation of the conundrum is to be part of a college or department that has increased in enrollment but has not actually increased net tuition revenue; in such cases faculty may find themselves being required to teach more students with the same number of faculty. Sometimes a smaller campus that adopts a curriculum revision to increase learning and save costs realizes it simply lacks the economy of scale to deliver a revised program effectively. Others face the paradox of unforeseen consequences when adopting technology as a way to teach more students efficiently.

Sometimes the stories faculty told dwelt on the realization that enrollment trends and cost factors align in troubling ways. This awareness at times gets expressed as anger at forces beyond their reckoning that bear down on them, other times as distress that nothing in their training or faculty experience has prepared them to address the challenges they face.

Finally, one of our recurrent observations from our more than 180 conversations with faculty members concerns a topic that was seldom mentioned explicitly, though it formed the context of many of our exchanges, much as a thick curtain might separate one part of a meeting room from a dark closet directly adjacent—that is, the prospect of solving the cost conundrum by growing smaller, leaving behind some things in order to create the discretionary space to pursue new initiatives and opportunities. Growing smaller in order to do what needs to be done better is "That Thing That Is Never Spoken Aloud." Only in a very few cases did we encounter voices giving expression to scenarios that reached beyond the veil in search of solutions to the cost conundrum.

THRESHOLDS OF UNSUSTAINABILITY

Although the conversations we had did not include the word "money" itself, they still conveyed that the faculty members were aware that the economy that makes possible their own programs of study requires a steady flow of enrollments. Enrollment is the coin of the realm, and anyone can recognize courses or majors that hover just above the threshold of unsustainability.

Sometimes the recognition of constraining horizons takes the form of a lament that a changing world has altered the motivations for students to become proficient in a foreign language; increasingly, the emphasis has come to center on learning language as a means of gaining cultural proficiency more than on learning language as a means of understanding the literature and history of another nation. With a touch of humor, one faculty member tells of the demise of what once was a great language tradition at her liberal arts college:

> We're now one big happy family of languages. "World Languages, Litera-
> tures, and Cultures" is the name of our department. WLLC, pronounced
> "we'll see." We think a lot about how short-sighted a lot of Americans are,
> believing, "Everybody in the world speaks English, so why would I need
> this?" And yet we as a college have set intercultural competence as one of
> our learning outcomes. I personally cannot think of a better way to learn
> that than to study another language and to study that culture by going
> there and living there and speaking the language and trying to make
> yourself understood. We're not the only ones who can offer that kind of
> experience, but I think we're the best ones to prepare students for that
> kind of thing. It is frustrating sometimes that we don't have more students
> majoring in a language. Of course, Spanish is a different matter; I think
> it's easier for most Americans to understand the utility of Spanish, and so
> many of our students are interested in preprofessional programs, in busi-
> ness or health professions, and so they see the utility. They wouldn't have
> to leave the U.S. at all to need Spanish; whereas it seems a little farther
> afield for them to learn Swedish or German.

Another language scholar expressed the impact of the cost conundrum in terms of the rigor of the department's expectations for its majors. She won-
ders, frankly, whether it does students a favor to encourage their continued enrollment if they are not progressing as needed:

I'm in the proficiency camp, meaning that I think that students should aim to continuously improve their proficiency in a language. I recognize that some people are not going to advance, and that may be OK for them. There are people who own businesses and do all of their work in a language. They have a heavy accent, their grammar is a mess, and there's a mixture of slang, but they function. Some of my colleagues tell me, "Well, if someone can function or it's not important for them to have that proficiency, that's OK. We want them to continue taking classes." For me, the problem is that we're always worried about enrollment. We don't want students to be discouraged and stop taking classes. We have very few students as French and German majors, so we'll lower all the barriers that might hinder retention of these students in our major. If they want to continue taking classes, that's wonderful. My problem with that, however, is that that's wonderful just like it's wonderful if I want to play softball. I'm terrible, but it might be fun for me. I shouldn't, however, be given some sort of certification that says, "You've completed x number of softball games, and therefore, you're certified by us as a sports major. You have our seal of approval for your abilities." That's the dilemma we're in right now. We want to encourage students to continue in an area but that means that when they finish, we say, "You're a major," and that's attached to an idea of proficiency.

In some cases, it's standards that get in the way; in others, it's logistics. In changing a pedagogy, a natural goal is to have all, or nearly all, the faculty of a program or department seek to improve the quality of their instruction, on the one hand, and their students' learning, on the other. But it is also the case that a new educational approach developed in a large university setting poses logistical problems in a smaller setting that doesn't benefit from the same economies of scale. Here is a faculty story in which a concept that has been appealing on educational grounds encounters a conundrum of cost in implementation:

We have two colleges that are extremely large, and another one that is large but online. We are the smallest college, so we're the little engine that could. The smaller colleges are having implementation issues with the modular math program we're currently piloting. The pilot is great, but if you're going to take a three-credit class and break it up into separate one-credit modules that students register for separately, you create a whole host of financial aid issues, enrollment issues, space issues, and veterans administration issues. Those things haven't been worked out yet, and the smaller schools stand to take more of a hit because we have to do everything the big schools do. We don't have six or seven separate classrooms to run these modules; our math department has, I think, a total of about five classrooms, and these have to handle all of the math classes, not just the developmental ones. It might be feasible in a department at a larger institution, where six or seven classrooms out of a dozen can be set aside to run modules. Another issue: What happens if a student has lined up modules 1, 2, and 3, and fails module 2? What do you do with that student for the last five weeks of the semester so that she or he can keep financial aid, continue to make progress, and not have to wait until the next semester? We came up with this idea of an emporium, which is a self-study experience, facilitated by a faculty member, where the student can try to finish up independently. Again, the implementation isn't pretty, even though the concept is great. We're at the point where the rubber meets the road, and for our small institution, it's all about being creative with limited resources.

A conversation with a physicist captured his exasperation with a budget model that effectively allows students to determine the allocation of funds in higher education departments. The time he spent as an administrator allowed him to put a theoretical gloss on the dilemma facing his colleagues. He is one of several people we spoke with who talked about the conundrum that comes from a shortage of students in one area, which then gives rise to an institution seeking compensating enrollments in another area rather than investing in a program that might solve the problem of an enrollment shortfall that started the discussion in the first place:

> One of the things that I began to understand as I did administrative work is that we actually allow students to dictate where we spend money. Where the students go, the money flows. You want students to go to STEM? Instead of allowing 780 majors in kinesiology here, cut it down to 400. Instead of having 875 business majors, cut it down to 500. Hire faculty, put up a building that has more classrooms, and what a shock, you'll have students majoring in STEM. It's even worse in our local community because in addition to STEM, we've got serious problems with anything related to social issues. Medical, we've got no health professionals in our area. We've got a lot of things we could really address, but it would take somebody who would really have to stir up a pot, right? I mean, because faculty have it in their heads that the way you get more money and make your department bigger and more important is to have more majors. That's just backwards. We are a state university funded by state funding, and we need to be able to deliver the goods in terms of having people who are needed to make our state function well. And don't think those departments don't have to change. I mean, the physics department

would, for example, have to understand that it needs to become more welcoming, so don't get me wrong, it's not just one-sided. It just seems to me wrong from an administrative point of view to run a tax-driven place and let the students decide where the money gets spent. That's just backwards.

Backward or not—it is the lesson faculty, when they think and talk about the financial constraints facing them, fall back upon almost every time. Another of our storytellers, who begins by describing the satisfaction of being a faculty member and having the freedom of a faculty member, highlights higher education's propensity to add without a corresponding reduction in other areas. In this case, the growth of student enrollment does not yield a better financial scenario for the department, because the larger number of enrolled students continues to be taught by essentially the same number of faculty as there were several years earlier:

> It is true that I'm a full professor and I've been here sixteen years. I feel very well paid for the work I do. The autonomy I have, the freedom and flexibility with my time are some of the things I value most.
>
> And still that's true—the opportunity to read what I want, research what I want, share with my students what I want, be involved in my volunteer work in the community. You know that colors my experience as a faculty member.
>
> I was sent a piece that I loved, said something like, "There is the irresistible urge to add new subjects reflecting the ever-expanding nature of the knowledge base while almost never deciding to take something else out." There's this increasing pressure to add, add, add, add, and for what, if we're not cutting something out? No wonder everybody's overdone.

Investments in technology can offer the prospect of greater efficiency, though they can also have the unforeseen consequence of increasing costs without a commensurate yield in either productivity or efficiency. Such investments are often conceived as a leading solution to the constraint of costs and creation of more efficient means of educating students. In the story that follows, the adoption of technology—offering a course online—also solves an enrollment problem, yielding full enrollment in a class that had been underenrolled in a traditional classroom format. But in this case, technology exacts its own toll on the cost equation, in the form of the increased time required to adapt a course to use materials from the internet that were produced for different purposes:

> In the computer and information science fields that I teach, there's been this student demand shift to online, and we're trying to cope with it. I

teach networking, which usually means crawling around on the floor, plugging in wires and configuring things, and now they want to take it online. The technology marketplace has responded some with simulated labs and stuff, but they don't work perfectly. Of course, things don't work perfectly in the real world either. For the first time, I had to take my income tax course and do it online because we haven't been able to fill the seats in class. Once we put it online, I've all of a sudden got a full class. But I will tell you, that was the first time I was trying to teach income tax online with open educational resources, and most of those materials are from the IRS, and they're written in legalese. I had to revert to open-study sessions on Tuesday nights. It wasn't easy. I'm going to revert back to a textbook with interpretations next time, which will save me from having to write a whole textbook. Also, there are stories behind the content in income tax, applications of "here's what this means." I'm going to record little lectures that round out the text, but I would much prefer to teach it face-to-face and get interactions with students about their experiences. Online was the only option because this course is a required course in one of the certificates in the local community, and we had to offer it at least once a year so that students could graduate. In the golden years, when there was lots of money, it was OK to get eight to ten students, but now that state aid has gone away and with budget tightening, students are not going to pay to have a class go with that few students in the seat. The class minimum is creeping up. It was ten to twelve; now it's pretty much fifteen.

Navigating Unfamiliar Terrain

A third group of faculty—after those who didn't talk about financial constraints to begin with and those for whom course and department enrollments were the singular financial indicators that mattered—was smaller in number. These were the faculty who had thought about the finances of their institution, knew what was and was not possible, and could speculate as to the relationship between costs and curricula. Collectively their stories attest to what might be possible if more faculty knew what these people knew—though we hasten to point out, this group of faculty was only marginally better at anticipating reform's unexpected consequences. Or to put the matter more directly, none of the stories we collected exhibited much financial prescience as to the economic consequences of reforming the undergraduate curriculum.

The faculty we talked with who had the best sense of the cost conundrum were those who had faced firsthand the unintended consequences of curricular reform efforts that had somehow gone astray. One of those who offered a "had we only known" lament told us that, in the end, it wasn't the shift from a teaching to a learning paradigm that was the problem but rather what the faculty didn't know enough about: the university's financial model.

One instance of curricular change we encountered was carried out with a principal concern for sustaining the vitality of the discipline—an instinct that is in full accord with the training, passion, and commitment of any faculty member. In this case, it was a recasting of requirements for the undergraduate major at the department level. The concern was to provide students with initial grounding in the traditions of the discipline as a prelude to further study. While the discussions were centered heavily on the value of the knowledge base and the primacy of students gaining critical insights into an extended tradition, the decision to change the curriculum was not devoid of practical consideration. In fact, the motivation was remarkably similar to that which caused a very different kind of institution to revamp its entire undergraduate curriculum:

> We had some declining enrollments. We were struggling, as most small, independent institutions do. When there are no vouchers from the state and no chance of vouchers from the state, you're constantly looking for where you can generate revenues. Student-generated revenues and student-generated income become essential. And when your enrollment's declining, it's like anything else. I do some consulting. If I go to a business that's making 12 percent profit a year and could be making 15 percent, but they would have to change, they're not that willing to listen. If they're three months from closing the doors, you tell them you've got to take some of your mother's hair and bury it in the backyard and things like that. We weren't at that level, but we recognized that for us to be competitive, we had to find something that gave us uniqueness and some distinction and allowed us to at least appear, from time to time, on the national stage or in national conversations. The switch to a learning paradigm with learning outcomes seemed like a way to become more distinctive. It also was a way to enhance learning, which seemed like a good thing to do.

In the case of the single department within a large university, the problem was less about enrollment decline in general than about disproportionate student interest in modern and contemporary literature with a corresponding decline from those interested in earlier historical periods. To create a better distribution of enrollments across all historical periods, members of the department chose to create a series of historical period courses, required of all majors. A core strategy was to make these historical courses team taught—a step that would introduce majors to a range of professors within the department, including some of the most talented and accomplished lecturers.

To agree on this course of action required considerable discussion in the department because of the inevitable trade-offs in determining which authors should be included within the historical offerings. This internal debate consumed time and emotional energy, and as one participant in the discussion recalls, the emphasis on the "what" of curriculum had largely precluded detailed considerations of financial or human costs in delivering the program they had designed:

> We were very well taken up by questions about curriculum. And we thought if the curriculum's good, we should do it. It's like that used up most of our bandwidth. And we didn't have the kind of emotional energy to do the kind of number crunching. And also you know these are political processes. When you try to get a department to move in any direction—political processes. I think we may have ended up making this more palatable by offering incentives to faculty to teach in the core that made a much larger burden.
>
> It made it over the longer term likely to be much more expensive. We didn't figure out the cost. I've never organized the curriculum for a year. I've never been curriculum director, so I'm not sure of all the details. But from what I understand, that is one of the major costs. When we did the literary history core and we committed to team teaching, which in many ways was a logical decision, it was a good idea. We have a lot of strong teachers. We're going to get every student who comes through our department to take this core. We want to showcase our teachers so that students can see, even if they're not immediately interested in, say, Chaucer, students could think, "Wow, there's this wonderful professor who gives a great series of lectures in medieval history; now I can go and take the course with her and she's going to be great." So I think we had the idea that it would be a kind of showcase for us, and it would help in the mildly beleaguered areas where there was underenrollment because we would be showing a lot of faculty to all our students.

As an intellectual principle and as a strategy to encourage a more balanced enrollment of majors across historical eras of literary achievement, the plan seemed sound. What it had not considered in full degree, however, were the costs that the new major exacted in terms of human energy, understood quite literally as staffing capacity as well as financial sustainability:

> But we didn't calculate that at the same time as we're doing literary history, we're also going to have these other requirements that we're going to have to commit to offer in each year. They'll also need to be taught by

faculty. An introductory class on poetry that has to be staffed each semester, and an introductory class on critical methods.

In simplest terms, the new structure for the major was one that added to an existing curriculum with very little corresponding reduction in earlier program offerings. Only one explicit requirement for the major was dropped:

Shakespeare, who had a kind of constituency anyway. And we've got some great Renaissance scholars here, and Shakespeare wasn't going to suddenly disappear off the radar screen. And students would be getting a lot of Shakespeare in the Renaissance and medieval first semester of the literary history sequence. The Shakespeareans didn't struggle tremendously about it. And I think it's actually been proved true that people still take Shakespeare classes. So we did do away with the Shakespeare requirement.

In addition to the internal debates of which authors the team-taught courses should highlight and what knowledge and capacities students should acquire from a recast major, the department had taken steps to gain external perspectives on its current offerings and its impact on its graduates:

We did a self-study or a sort of disciplinary study. I worked with a statistician that we found from the medical school, and we wanted to find what's happened with our majors over time, what's happening to the discipline nationally with majors, what is happening in relation to other majors at this institution, and which things are our students actually studying. We didn't know anything really about what our students were doing, or if we did, it was all kind of anecdotal. There were no hard numbers at all. So we did a pretty solid statistical analysis, and that was another important consciousness-raising factor, I think. We could actually see what was happening, and some of the things that we found were worrying if you believe that it is important for a major to retain as many students as possible. In an institution, it's hard to argue against that, just in terms of billets and general influence of the university.

So we tried to understand who we were and where we were within the university, within the discipline as a whole. We did some charts and graphs and numbers, so we had the self-study. We had student focus groups and then a lot of discussions.

As I said, we made decisions that were profligate in terms of faculty resources, but I feel like we tried to go as far as we could in making this a rational process. We didn't get the whole way. We probably could have done better in hindsight, but, you know, just moving a department of our size, and I wouldn't say fractiousness, because generally it's quite a collegial department most of the time. But moving us all in a different direction with implications for all of us about what we'd be teaching—that's no easy thing to do.

So I think it was definitely a good faith effort, and if we found out things subsequently that we hadn't thought about, some of them were unforeseen, and some of them we just couldn't assimilate or metabolize at the time. Also, you know we're an English department, and we haven't really dealt in statistics, in numbers and plans, very much. It's been construed as being kind of antithetical to who we are. If we were having a similar discussion today, I think we would be more open to just kind of trying to figure it out like a math problem.

Figuring it out like a math problem is something that faculty members of almost any discipline find hard to do. What troubled most of the scholars featured in this chapter was a sense of being in over their heads. The curriculum and pedagogy they understood well enough; what they lacked was language and a tool kit for asking the key financial and resource questions.

One of the most tenacious elements of the cost conundrum for faculty in general is the reluctance to apply the full array of functions a mathematics tool kit can supply—namely, the act of subtraction. The possibility of reduction is one that virtually no one trained for a career in the academy entertains willingly. On the one hand, everyone understands the basic equation, and the prospect of reducing course offerings or reducing staff because of enrollment declines can motivate inspired strategies to maintain current resources and allocations. On the other hand, when the relationship between program offerings and course enrollments becomes unsustainable, there is a reluctance to speak openly in frank financial terms. In one case we heard, academic training in a quantitative field, combined with experience as a faculty trustee, fortified one person's resolve to speak plainly about the institution's continued financial well-being, even while knowing the risk of being frank:

I serve on our board of trustees. I also serve on strategy and planning. Do I constantly put in plugs for "This is what we should be doing as a good business model"? Yes. Is it often listened to? No. Twenty years ago, I left another liberal arts college where five students less in enrollment would make all the difference in the world in whether it survived that year or needed to get out. We are not in those dire straits because our endowment is pretty good and we weathered some really bad storms over the years. But it is a constant problem. Right now, we're spending more than we take in, and I keep talking to our president about setting the enrollment target according to what reasonable number of admissions we can get and not on what the budget needs, but we once again have a very high enrollment target this year. In a state where the number of high school graduates keeps dropping every year, I always hear, "Well, we go out of state." And I say, "Yes, we recruit a lot in the Midwest, but they're facing the same thing we are." We need to start setting targets based on what we can get and then budget accordingly. All the programs we have on this campus are good if we had the money, but we're not in good times.

I don't care what the discount rate is. The question should be, "What's the net revenue per student?" If we actually reduce the net revenue per student but increase the number of students, now we're into economics and elasticity, and depending on where the trade-offs are, we could be in better shape; we can be in worse shape. I don't know if this conversation takes place on other boards, but it does on ours. We've had consultants come in and tell us to drop the discount rate. Our most recent consultant said to "up" the discount rate. And it's a trade-off. If I up the discount rate, my net revenue per student is down. Unless I increase students, the total revenue to the college is down. Our costs are going up, and we're in that vicious spiral again. We are one of the few industries—health care is also an exception—where our prices have gone up far in excess of inflation over the last twenty years, and we are refusing to address why our costs are going up in excess of inflation. I will hear it is salaries. Well, no, corporate America has that pressure. It is utilities; corporate America has that pressure. It is financial aid. OK, that's part of it, but that's funny money. It's going in; it's coming out. That's not the reason.

We need to address all of our expenditures and determine whether we really need all these programs. I'm a faculty member, and I can get myself shot. In the last five years, we have offered new programs in nursing, health care administration, and biotechnology, and we have hired new faculty for those positions. Meanwhile, our total enrollment has stayed constant. Well, if our total enrollment has stayed constant and we are gaining majors in these fields, we are losing majors in other fields. Now no, I am not mean enough to say we should go out and fire faculty. That is not what I'm proposing. What I am proposing is when we have a retirement, we should really look at that position and ask, "Do we replace it?" Again, it's a zero-sum game, and if I'm gaining in one place, I'm losing in another.

It is a soliloquy that includes the basics that matter most—the focusing on the discount rate instead of honing in on net revenue per student, the depressing realization that flat enrollments must limit the ability of an institution to offer new programs unless it is also prepared to close underenrolled ones, and the fact, as he put it, that he could get himself shot for pointing out that in order to add faculty, you have to simultaneously subtract faculty in departments with flat enrollments.

Another instance of a faculty member who ventured to speak plainly about curriculum and cost is a declaration that recounts important themes offered in this chapter. This passage echoes the earlier lamentation about allowing student choice to dictate the allocation of funds in an institution while also voicing concern that a department that caters excessively to student tastes will bolster enrollment by diluting the rigor of study in its major. The price of maintaining fidelity to the core principles of a discipline may be a department that is academically strengthened—though smaller in size:

> It seems to me that the biggest problem for literature departments . . . is how to make history interesting to students. Because let's face it, English departments are trying to survive by becoming more and more twentieth-century American culture departments. I think part of this is inevitable. Fine. But as an intellectual policy, I think it's wrong. You know, literature is an object of study whose greatest treasure by far is in the past. How do you make the past interesting for young people who are extremely taken by the present, especially in the current generation for obvious reasons with the digital acceleration of everything, et cetera?
>
> Do I see this department or any other English department I know addressing this issue in a way? Honestly, no. Because addressing it seriously may mean losing even more students. You know, if you really want to be a department that cares about history, you're probably going to lose another 30 percent or 50 percent of your majors. I think this would be a good idea. OK, we will lose five faculty positions, ten faculty positions. Fine. It would be just a realistic assessment of who it is who really wants to study literature.

This statement is a penetrating critique of what student preferences and the economics of survival have cost the scholarly enterprise. It is offered by one who is admittedly nearing retirement but who nonetheless does not shy away from the consequences of his argument. To maintain the integrity and strength of the discipline, he proposes that a department should be willing to pay the price, though in truth, it is his younger colleagues who would have to absorb the cost of doing so.

Getting beyond the Conundrum: A Primer on Curriculum and Costs

In a range of institutional and disciplinary contexts, our conversations repeatedly underscored the need for faculty members to gain a more substantial understanding of costs in the institutions and departments they inhabit. No one can blame faculty for lacking proficiency in realms for which they received no training in graduate school or in their careers as faculty members.

But a basic understanding of the finances of a university or college—of revenues, expenditures, and factors that inform decisions about the allocation of resources to fulfill institutional mission—needs to be part of every faculty member's basic realm of understanding, regardless of academic discipline.

As scholars and analysts—and, yes, as consultants—the three of us have spent a quarter century or more, independently or in concert, serving as advisors to institutions undertaking strategic plans or other initiatives that encourage faculty members and their administrative colleagues to imagine a future for their institution that combines visionary thinking with practical considerations of what is feasible. Strategic planning, in the broadest sense, is an exercise that involves faculty in understanding an institution's market position, endowment size, donor base, and practical ability to achieve academic goals for the years and decades ahead. As outsiders and facilitators, we observe that engaging in strategic planning is an exercise in connecting institutional aspirations with a realistic understanding of what is possible to achieve. Through a sequence of conversations and practical trade-offs extending over a year or more, a key benefit of such a process is the education it gives to an academic community about the ways in which institutional visions align with resources to become reality.

A faculty that understands the important connection between institutional vision and its achievement—or more specifically, between curriculum and costs—is one that we believe is better prepared to transcend the cost conundrum and to make collective choices as members of a campus community with a fuller understanding of what is entailed in the choices made.

Just as enlightening as a strategic planning process, it is possible to enhance faculty understanding of costs through workshops that instill a basic understanding of how institutions work from both a political and cost perspective. There are many organizations and groups that offer such basic training, and without advocating any program in particular, it is worth recounting statements from a recent evaluation by faculty participants in one such program. The question on the evaluation asked faculty participants to say what they had learned from the three-day primer in costs, academic leadership, and negotiation. The responses attest to the benefits that can result from providing a general introduction to decision-making in negotiation scenarios involving role-playing combined with exercises that include inventing a hypothetical institution and making it financially sustainable:

- I know better now what questions I should ask to get information I need in order to lead well.
- I gained a broader and deeper perspective on issues and challenges colleges face.

- I learned where and when to give up and when to be assertive.
- I gained confidence that I can handle being a chair.
- I learned to go beyond the specific problem and think more broadly of related issues.
- I learned that many, many things should be taken into consideration when dealing with different personalities and complex situations.
- I learned about the big picture—sacrificing battles to win the war.
- I learned that trust is important—and the need to maintain collegiality.

Comments of this kind from faculty members who are trained in a discipline but have not thought that much about the elements of cost or decision-making in their institution give grounds for hope. Faculty members are quick studies; they cannot have attained the positions they hold without a sustained commitment to learn and expand their understanding. As the president of one Midwestern university has said, "There are many ways to get to California"—which is to say, many ways for an institution or department to achieve its academic and strategic goals. Part of the passage beyond the cost conundrum is simply to instill in faculty a better understanding of how revenues and costs inform decision-making in their own institutions.

Faculty Voice

Redesigning curricula is like pulling teeth, as this storyteller attests. The chief academic officer of a large public university, he spearheaded a major overhaul that was years and years in the making. It was finally worth it, but it took a number of different design groups and processes to pull it off. It also demanded sustained effort to make the politics turn out in the university's favor.

The new general education program has been very well received. By the end of the process, when we had to have a vote, it only ended up having one dissenting vote. So it was well received by the end. The process was very transparent and offered many opportunities for people to take part in the dialogue. We did have one attempt at the twenty-third hour to subvert the program with the complaint, "Well, we didn't know about it." We were able to show that that was not the case, and a number of people jumped into the conversation and supported that. So by the time it went up for a series of votes, we were very pleasantly surprised that it got all the support it did.

We started out with a large group of faculty and staff who volunteered to be part of this process. Not all of them volunteered because they were in support of this; they wanted to keep an eye on it, yes, but what we got out of that group after three years was passage of the student learning outcomes and a framework to go forward. We then moved on to a different process and created two teams, one very large one and one small leadership team of people who were very committed to the process. We worked over one summer in particular and got a lot of work done with a lot of discussion, some of it very intense, but by the end of that summer, we were in pretty good shape, and it took us until the following spring to get it through. As I said, being very transparent was important.

The one lesson I learned along the way was that we didn't have to get every single senior faculty member on board. We had a good group of senior leadership involved, but some of the junior faculty—who were looking at their future on campus and had more invested and knew what was going to happen—took a leading role. They were able to get over the final hurdles, I think, easier than some of the others would have from the first group that we put together. They went out and visited every single department and division that we had and talked it through. We dealt with objections that different departments had, and there were many, most of which were turf based. "Are we going to lose this or that?" And we said, "No, you won't lose anything if you make the transition." I think the only thing that ended up being eliminated was a one-credit physical education piece, and most of that was already being taught online anyway.

The faculty were really excited about what we were going to do, and last year we implemented it. Most of it was good, but if you don't plan it all out, you just can't assume these people are going to walk into the classroom and know what to do, so we've had some bumps along the way. We have a fantastic group of people called the "obstacle team" that meets weekly and has been great as boots-on-the-ground people who are looking into the bumps. The transfer process has been one of the issues that has required a lot of tweaking and a couple more people in place to help with the logistics. We have also been a little overly ambitious in terms of the pressure that it puts on advisors and other areas that we take for granted like peer and alumni mentors. We're looking at these things.

We've had different people involved during different phases of the process. The first process was not only dealing with pedagogy, but it was also a very political process, which took us a little while longer than the chancellor had hoped. On the other hand, he was delighted with the results and couldn't believe the scope of the change that was involved. So he was glad that he stuck with us and waited, and certainly we're going to be in a position with our next accreditation review to say a lot of good things.

Now we're starting with the community engagement piece of the program when all of our second-year students go out and work with community members. So far that's received a lot of exciting press and good reviews, but again, we're still working on the infrastructure. I gave two-year contracts to a lot of people to see what we are going to need short term and long term. Right now, I think we're at least one faculty member short, who I need to bring over and get involved in administration to support people who are a little overburdened. Also, we certainly didn't anticipate that our program would be so successful that our director would be raided, and at the last moment, to boot. That was a critical juncture, and honestly, it would have been very difficult if we hadn't had someone here who could step right in and the faculty trusted. They had bought in, but they bought in with a certain group of people, and it would have been very difficult at that point to bring someone in from the outside.

It's taken us forty years to get this revised general education program into place, not ten years. We've been told every ten years by our accreditors that we have to do something. They said the last time they were here that we had even made general education worse than their time before. So I think people were ready, but we had to move them away from checklists, boxes. That's why that first group had to stop after three years. What really helped was when the first group presented its findings, and all three or four of their options involved checking the boxes. It was almost unanimous from the people who were in the audience that day that none of the options were sufficient. That presentation gave us the energy, I think, that we needed, and we brought it through, and we brought it through slowly. I'm not sure all the faculty—or anyone—understood what this revision was going to entail, but once they got involved with changing their courses and writing new courses, it was very interesting. We have a very senior faculty member who is a "you have to prove it to me" kind of person. He didn't think this was going to work at all, and he taught the first semester of the new program and came away so excited about the possibilities. His wife also teaches on campus, and she said, "Oh, it's changed our lives." He's much more energized now and is really excited about what he's doing. We never thought we'd get a convert from that group.

Faculty Voice

Touching the Third Rail

Having served his college as both a faculty member and senior administrator for more than twenty-six years, he now fears that difficult conversations are becoming more veiled, particularly when the task at hand is designing a new set of distribution requirements. He is equally worried about the silence in the classroom from students who have been schooled in conflict avoidance. His story tackles this concern, but it also talks about his belief that learning is no longer based on what students come to know but rather how they learn it. He feels that content can be gained anywhere, but its usage requires engagement through experiential learning and other forms of pedagogy.

The discussion the faculty had about distribution requirements was a lot of time spent on something that ultimately was, I believe (and this is a minority opinion), an attempt to legislate diversity through distribution requirements. I think it's a noble effort, but I don't really think it gets down at the ground level and deals with the issues as comprehensively as they might be. One of the things that was interesting to me as an "Americanist" listening to the faculty debate was that there was this kind of discussion as to what constitutes North America. Should the United States be included? People got up and started talking about how it turns out that, in fact, there is a lot of diversity in the United States, and we really ought to pay attention to that. Just because America is part of North America doesn't mean we aren't also engaging and promoting issues of global understanding.

When we talk about curricular innovation, that conversation about distribution was an old-fashioned conversation because we were talking about content, or at least we thought we were talking about content. We weren't really talking about how people learn and how we engage our students. And over the last year or so when these issues of diversity—racial differences—came to the surface, we talked about how the press is full of stories about macroaggressions and trigger warnings and so on. To me, what these stories are saying to us is that we need to spend more time talking about how we engage the various students that are coming to our classrooms. You can teach a class that spans the world in terms of content, but if you're not engaging students in a particular way, it doesn't really make much difference.

The last couple of years, I team-taught a course with a faculty member who's an ecologist, and I'm in American Studies. We taught this course called—and this is somewhat innovative, I suppose—"Across the Great Divide: Science, Humanities, and the American Landscape." We did four modules and tried to show changes over time and to look at crisis points and tried to bring science and humanities into the classroom. Our final module was on Katrina, and we showed a film that included a lot of handheld cameras showing an African American family in the midst of flooding. This wasn't the famous Spike Lee film, which we showed this year, but this film was sort of . . . well, the students found it disturbing.

When we talked about the film afterwards and started to engage in issues of African American identity and how people in the Ninth Ward were handling the flood and so on and so forth, it was really striking to us that the students who were primarily white couldn't talk about it. They were almost paralyzed. I mean, they said things like, "We can't really imagine what the experience of a poor African American is." We got notes from some of the students after the class, saying, "We should pause and talk about this." And we did.

I think it was really worthwhile, but I was struck by how carefully you need to pave the way to having discussions of topics that I, as a fifty-eight-year-old person, would have thought we could have. The positive reading here is that our well-intentioned white students were wary of having these conversations because they knew that they couldn't possibly see the world as someone else saw it, but I think the real reason they couldn't have these conversations was because they were so highly attuned to their subject positions. They've been well trained not to have the conversation, and that's a real barrier to education. No matter what kind of students you're talking to, you have to get everyone to a place where they're engaging this stuff together. I mean, that's what we do as educators, right?

So this year before we saw the Spike Lee film, I actually sent an email out to the students. I basically said, "Maybe this is something of a trigger warning, but I just want you to know that the film that we're going to be watching has some disturbing imagery. You'll see this and you'll see that. So let's come to class prepared to talk." And that helped. Of course, it was a completely different course, and who knows if it was even necessary to send out the email.

I'm further on in my career, I guess, and I have less faith that content is going to get us where we want to go. It's how we do the work in the classroom. I have been thinking about this stuff quite a bit, and some of my work administratively has been to support the development of digital learning. I have become more and more interested in the possibility of using a digital way to get into some of these difficult issues. The thing I think we sometimes forget, even at a place like this, where we value face-to-face teaching so much, is that it ultimately really does come down to how we teach. I mean, you can get content anywhere, but you have to finally bring it down to where the students get it.

CHAPTER 7

Barriers

WHAT IS AS TRUE now as it was in the 1980s, as reflected in the ire of *Integrity in the College Curriculum*, is that changing what and how faculty teach is roughly akin to running an obstacle course. There are barriers everywhere, for the most part faculty made, and at the same time the curriculum itself is constantly expanding as faculty add more courses, create more majors, and specify more options. The result is an undergraduate experience that continues to lack coherence and an institutional context that is rapidly becoming financially unsustainable.

One of the more telling of our conversations was with a longtime faculty member at a liberal arts college that had stumbled. Having promised to implement a senior project in an effort to reimpose curricular coherence, the college subsequently found it couldn't, even though its administration had funded a substantial number of additional faculty positions to support the initiative:

> We tried to imagine how something like the senior project would fit into the sciences curriculum, and we just couldn't find a way to make it seem meaningful. So yeah, there were some very passionate, eloquent, sometimes angry speeches on the faculty floor saying we committed to this, and we believe in it, and other people saying, "We believe in it too, but it's going to be so watered down, we're going to have students doing a book report and calling that a meaningful senior project. And we don't think that is . . . that's not what it is in the sciences."
>
> We voted it down. The faculty voted it down, and I think the administration was beside itself. I think from a faculty perspective, we haven't always understood where the faculty lines are going and what the rationale for them is because we have added faculty. And we heard that from the president time and time again, "You have your new faculty lines and now you're still not doing it." We said, "But we don't have them in the places where we need them." The curriculum committee, which is a faculty committee, are the ones who were deciding where the lines went,

based on the budget given to them, so this wasn't an administration versus the faculty situation. We have a faculty committee. But I'm just not sure that the decisions were being made over that seven- to eight-year period with senior work in mind. There might have been other enrollment pressures or other goals in mind.

It is a scenario that exemplifies the tragedy of the commons: every individual decision is rational and well thought out and makes complete sense, and of course it was the right decision. But ten decisions later, the effect is one of impoverishment. It is a lesson echoed in many of our stories—the gnawing sense that their colleges and universities are being overwhelmed by too many good things accompanied by a hindered ability to choose among them. Along with an abundance of good ideas, there have been too many earnest arguments, committees that couldn't make decisions, faculty meetings that exacerbated rather than resolved issues or solved problems, convoluted bureaucracies that are no longer trusted, and processes and procedures the faculty itself put in place that turned out to have made change nearly impossible.

Talking without Listening

We were struck by how easily the faculty with whom we talked enumerated these problems. What many stories shared in common was a sense of frustration that initiatives they wanted to pursue as individuals were too seldom brought to fruition. They evoke settings in which discourse occurs and many points are shared, which nonetheless lead to no change in thinking or commitment to alter the existing order. There is talk a-plenty but little listening and less change. A frequent complaint was how difficult it proved to get help from one's disciplinary and programmatic neighbors. The story that follows, about the struggles of a program in health care at a liberal arts college, quietly reflects the kinds of disappointment that many, perhaps even a majority of faculty, now feel. The account begins by citing a team of marketing consultants who perhaps knew better than the faculty what was really holding their college back:

> I keep coming back to a conversation that we had with our most recent marketing consultants who came in to help us develop this new branding initiative. This was a group that had worked with some of the top liberal arts institutions in the country. I will never forget it. We were sitting there in the focus group, and one of my colleagues from the sciences said, "You keep responding as we're describing our programs; you keep telling us how wonderful these programs are. You've worked with the best liberal arts colleges across this country. If we have all these great programs, could you tell us why we don't have the same reputation that those institutions

have?" And I will never forget the answer. Their response was, "You have wonderful individual programs, but they are exactly that. They are isolated programs, and there is no coherence. They do not come together to basically create a common vision, a common mission from the programming."

I have seen this. Three years ago, I stepped in as we were developing an integrative health studies program. This was to be a signature program bringing faculty from all three disciplines together to create curricular programming and career development programming that would change the way we were doing undergraduate education for students interested in pursuing health. It was health care delivery, but it was also health policy, health care administration. And after three years of working with that, we did some very nice things with the career development and preparation piece, but we made very, very little progress on the rest of that curricular development of interdisciplinary programming. The integrated health program was working, and we were trying desperately to bring students from political science, sociology, communication, and then the basic sciences together. We had students who were sitting in the program while we also had our public affairs program. Students were doing and working on the same projects, but we could not get these two programs—the public affairs program and our curricular programming—to intersect. And I think it's the best example of our inability to do that.

Contributing to that inability are a host of philosophical arguments that never get settled, as in the argument about the validity of interdisciplinary majors:

Some faculty don't like our interdisciplinary majors because they have a valid argument in that a major is supposed to give you depth in a discipline and liberal education is supposed to give you breadth. How do we now have these interdisciplinary majors when the students don't really even have a discipline? It's a really good argument because the way to become interdisciplinary is that I have a discipline and someone else has a different discipline. We come together to solve a problem. That's how you know it's considered interdisciplinary. Is it possible or even logical for me to become interdisciplinary, meaning can I get enough depth in this and enough depth in something else that I can then start linking them and become interdisciplinary? And that's the argument or the question. Some faculty don't want to give up the idea that there can be learning and value in an interdisciplinary major.

In describing this sense of insularity and resistance to new thinking on how to structure programs of learning, the faculty member in this story drew circles with her fingers to portray how separated faculty interests had become:

Well, the issue is that there are sound barriers around these individual circles. People are willing to talk, but they're not willing to listen. And if we could get people to say, "Well, let me allow you to speak; let me process the information you're giving me, do some synthesis of that information; let me even do something as simple as repeat it back to you to make sure that I'm hearing exactly what you're sending over to me and then formulate my questions to send back," then we'd be able to move these circles closer together. But right now, we don't do that well here.

A more aggressive variation on the practice of simply ignoring what others say is to listen with the sole intention of calling out elements to attack in others' statements—as in a search-and-destroy mission:

I think we're a deeply conservative faculty, small *c* conservative, so when there's a problem, we're quick to highlight the problem. And we're also quick to shoot down every posed solution in sequence. So any change is immediately shot down as problematic while at the same time focusing on the fact that the status quo is also a problem. Even amongst the group that wants change, wants to work together, there is this deep conservatism that change is scary, so let's immediately poke holes in any proposal before it even gets out of the gate even though we recognize that something has to change. Something has to give. So a couple of members of the group who are trying to identify ways to change are saying, "Can we please just throw ideas out there without people shooting them down right away? OK, what can we do to reinvigorate academic life so that the college isn't on a slow bleed?" We're not going under anytime soon, but we're losing what we were.

Scattered throughout these faculty stories of academic decision-making processes are touches of humor, some intended, some not. One description provides a whimsical account of those who become victims of the aggressive listening tactics previously described. It is also a story about the role longevity used to play in organizing faculty interests. Here it helps to remember something about carnival games:

My sense of the past, before I came, was that there was a faculty voice, but it was the voice of, say, five individuals who were well understood to be "the voice," and what they said is what was done. Since I've been here, there's been a move away from that sort of thing, and there's a very strong egalitarian feel. I end up characterizing it as a Whack-a-Mole kind of situation where if someone sticks their head up too much, they get whacked down. If a group tries to move in a certain direction, there tends to be an inertia pulling back.

Several offered vignettes of the formal faculty meeting as a venue for a decision-making process that is ostensibly democratic and deliberative but something different and less inclusive in actual practice:

I think that there's a great deal to be said about a careful, deliberative, slow process whereby change is debated. We're not in a crisis situation where we need to make long-term decisions right now, but I do believe that there are ways in which we can grease the wheels to make change happen a little more quickly. At this point there's apathy, disgust, frustration, resignation among many faculty members that depresses the vote in faculty meetings. It means that people don't feel as though they are invested, listened to. Older faculty tend to be the ones who turn up, and older faculty, especially much older faculty, tend to be the ones who speak at faculty meetings. The great objection is that a small coterie of faculty dominates these meetings, and I think it's off-putting to those who don't speak, who feel intimidated for a wide variety of different reasons. It's not a good venue to make changes to legislation. It's terrible. It should be used to raise issues of great moment.

The second characteristic of a faculty meeting that slows and frustrates the process of decision-making is the need for all players to feel full ownership, even if they have had no role in the work of researching and shaping a proposal for policy action:

At every faculty meeting that we have, we go through the exact same practices. So the first item gets introduced in a very defensive manner by the administrators. Lots of contextualization as to why it wasn't motivated by them and it wasn't motivated by the faculty. Here are the conditions why we're making this change. Here's what we're looking at; here's the research. We need to have these conversations. And then the questions start from the faculty. And the questions immediately demonstrate that there is resistance, that there is defensiveness, that there is suspicion, and this has to go on for several different meetings, and it's exactly the same pattern on every issue. And then after the discussions and the same questions have been asked multiple times with exactly the same answers coming back, then the faculty members show an interest and then there are congratulations—"Wow, we're doing a really good job. Wow, this feels like this is the right thing. This is a good thing. We really need to make this decision." And then the faculty make the decision, and we move on to the next issue. The faculty make the decisions, but there's this immediate suspicion. So they have to go through this process of "Let me ask the critical questions to reveal this underlying agenda. Oh, there's not an underlying agenda."

LOOPINESS

Ultimately, we concluded that what these faculty were talking about was something we had come to recognize as process addiction:

> A lot of professors feel that there's got to be a structure for everything. We're very fixated on what the exact process is, what the right procedure is, drawing up all the plans and having everything exactly perfect before we go forward. What's the problem if we dip our toe in the water and then figure out how we're actually going to swim? That might be better than waiting until we actually know or waiting until we realize that we don't know.

What this faculty member is referring to is the almost endless process of recycling—of the advance and retreat of arguments that confronts anyone wanting to change something, whether big or small. It is a condition we came to describe as "loopiness." Even at the smallest institution we visited, and certainly at the largest, the enumeration of the processes and structures involved in the making of curricular decisions was as complex as it was seemingly endless. Here it helps to lay out something of a structural map beginning with the academic department. A good example of an issue that is replicated everywhere—big university, small college, community college—is told by a liberal arts college professor of long standing. He had set out with a prospectus he had developed in conjunction with like-minded colleagues wanting to set up an interdisciplinary major with a relatively loose structure that drew its courses from a cluster of five social science departments:

> OK, so we do that, and we come up with a cluster of courses that we think are going to do that. Then the question becomes, How do we get the flexibility from our departments to allow us to actually teach those courses? That's going to play out very differently depending on the department. There are some departments where the idea of teaching a course outside of their area is welcome because their enrollments are so bad that this is a way to draw students in. Other departments have no flexibility whatsoever. For example, econ cannot spare anyone because there is too much demand on econ for their core curriculum. So that's one major obstacle there.
>
> So it's really hard to see how we would change the structures of our curriculum and our staffing to enable us to share competencies and literacy across our departmental structure in order to get our students to think in more interdisciplinary ways. So I think that realistically, most faculty say, "Well, these are really hard questions, and the college is doing pretty well, my major is doing OK—I can keep doing what I'm

doing and I don't need to grapple with that." And even those of us who want to blow things up recognize that you can only blow so much up at one time.

Departments are relatively mushy obstacles that can change or not change simply by installing a new chair or through a cluster of retirements followed by a supply of new appointments. Much harder targets are committees, which more often than not are hardwired into faculty governance as described in the faculty handbook:

> I have served on so many big committees where we are assigned a task. You know, it's a committee formed by faculty. They pick us and they give us the task, and then we go off and do the task. And a couple of committees I've been on I've worked for two or three years on a task. And then we bring it back. In the interim, it's not like we just go off by ourselves and go in a cave, you know?
>
> We have meetings; we have forums.
>
> We send them emails, we ask them to read stuff, we ask for writing—we do the whole spiel. And then we bring this product and then they go, "Have you thought about this? Nobody asked me." And we're like, "Shut up, are you kidding?" It's just like you can almost predict. I always tell my husband, "I can just lay money on it. Like you know we're going to present next week, and I can tell you who's going to say it and what they're going to say."
>
> And then it gets shot down or either dies or barely squeaks by, and you don't have buy-in, and then it's going to fail, because people will just go in their classroom, shut the door, and do whatever the heck they want.
>
> And it's eternally frustrating. I think it's trust. I really think that we do not really trust each other's professionalism, and we don't really trust each other to not be selfish, you know? To consider the whole.

BONDS OF TRADITION

This absence of trust is often exacerbated by the fact that comparatively few faculty members can commit the same degree of diligence and expertise to committee work that they devote to their own research. Time is no less of a problem. Often faculty serve but never give adequate time to the work of the committees on which they serve. It is a satisficing solution—no one is really happy, and the result is what this historian described as clumsy solutions:

> Committees I've been on, everybody's very busy, which means we come to meetings unprepared. We lack the ability to go do the research that one would normally want to do to be up to speed on the issues. Many of us

lack just the basic mental apparatus for understanding some of this. We're not economists. For most of my years in higher education, I just didn't understand how a college works, and I've only recently begun to see how a college works from a different point of view than just as a historian in a department. I realize, "Oh, my gosh, a college is a six-ring circus, and we're just part of one little ring." I used to think we *were* the college. Yeah, boy, did I have an education about that. It's frustrating. We're trying to solve a really hard problem, and we don't have enough knowledge or time to grapple with it very well, so we come up with clumsy solutions.

Another story about committee work is one that cuts both ways, told by the chair of a communications department who also happened to chair her college's curriculum committee. She begins by explaining what she and her departmental colleagues wanted and why, despite the fact that she chaired the committee, the department did not win the battle:

> In order for us to change our major, it has to go through the Educational Policy Committee. We submitted it three times to that committee, which I chair, and I couldn't get the faculty to budge on accepting the changes. There is a tradition here of a thirty-six-credit major. We wanted our major to be thirty-six course credits, plus a four-credit internship. So it's a forty-credit major, and it couldn't pass.
>
> What we wanted to do was to keep the same amount of credits in the major but get rid of the required cognates in order to try to make the major as flexible as possible. In other words, we wanted to keep the same number of credits. The students would take the same number of credits, but rather than prescribing what the cognates need to be, the students would be able to choose them. And we did that because we wanted to try to work with individual students to craft the path through the major that makes sense given, within reason, what their goals or interests are. All the students need to learn how to think critically. They need to understand how to analyze data at some basic level, even though they don't really want to necessarily take a statistics class. If they want to do any kind of audience analysis, that is going to be part of what they need to learn. So there's the broccoli, right? You have to get your vegetables somewhere in our major, but how can we give them the cheese sauce that makes it worthwhile?
>
> The committee would not vote, even though our major was going from fifty-two credits to forty credits. The committee would not vote on that because it remained forty credits within the major, not that we were trying to increase the number of credits in the major, but because it remained at forty credits in the major.

I know; it doesn't make any sense. It's not that our faculty couldn't see the logic in the decision, but they felt bound by tradition to not approve the changes to the communication major even though we were creating a more flexible system that was going to be better for our students and reduce the overall number of prescribed courses that they needed to take within our major.

There are two ways to interpret this story. In the storyteller's view, what was at stake was the kind of flexibility that a rapidly changing knowledge base required in the modern era. What she is advocating is a kind of "just in time" college curriculum. You won't know what you need to study until you have first spent time working through the basics of your major—in this case, communications and media studies.

The second perspective, implied but not directly voiced in this account, is the underlying force driving the committee members' resistance. What she wants her students to be excused from is a predetermined set of required cognates from other disciplines. And that is the rub. It is the expected enrollments in other departments that she is trifling with, eliminating, in the process, the near certainty that the economics department, for example, will know the minimum number of students it would have to teach. In this case, the committee structure was used to filibuster a curricular change that in many respects made perfect educational sense.

In fact, it often happens that an effort to simplify the curriculum runs afoul of some faculty member's interest in preserving the status quo as a means of holding on to departmental enrollments:

> The discussion is partially about maintaining coherency in the curriculum and partially about our previous iteration of general education, which had the upper division divided into twenty-three themes. With the redesign, there was a turf war, with some people being very concerned that they were going to lose their major cash cows that were supporting their program. It was really kind of vicious for a while, with people working to get their courses to fit into some pathway. With so many limitations, that was difficult.

In larger institutions in general and multicampus community colleges in particular, the alternative to the kind of faculty committees previously described is what might best be called a learning bureaucracy. In some cases these function as arbiters of standardization in courses of the same title taught at different campuses of a system. Another function of systemic decision-making bodies is to define what constitutes a reasonable teaching load within disciplines. The more pronounced the differences among different divisions, the more likely there will be plenty of opportunities for insidious comparisons:

> The faculty curriculum committee outlined for the chairs some of their decision-making criteria about new lines: "Because enrollment pressures are huge, give us numbers." And I said, "So with regard to enrollments, the enrollments per FTE, you're saying that's an important criterion." And they said, "Yes." And I said, "Well, how does that explain last year's positions? Because they had some in the languages, and the languages are at thirty-five students per FTE or something like that. All the bunch of science departments were one hundred and whatever per FTE." And they said, "Well, oh, well, the sciences are different." And I said, "Well, what do you mean they're different?" "Well, they don't need the small class sizes that the languages do and that math does." And I said, "According to whom?" "Well, the divisions are just not all going to be the same." I said, "But why? Because all the educational literature I read in the STEM fields make the same arguments and have the same data to support that. We also need smaller class sizes instead of having an eighty-five-person chemistry class and physics class and biology class."

Angry Voices, Awkward Absurdities

Mixed in the stories were touches of remorse and even anger, reflecting in some cases that an outcome might have been different if one had exerted more effort to bringing about a desired curriculum change. Occasionally there were expressions of more palpable anger by those who felt that certain goals advanced by an institution were more for show than for sustained action. Some instances of this anger stemmed from those who promoted diversity on campus. The most common charge was that their administrations were all talk and no action. Often those comments centered on the curriculum and the absence of faculty of color:

> When the accreditation people came, it was like, "OK, multicultural and gender studies, put on your tap shoes; you've got a show to do." Then once they left, we felt that we'd be taken care of, but they're just like, "Wait, y'all are where? Who's that?" There's been nobody hired; there are three of us who have joint appointments there, but it's nobody's home department. This office that we're meeting in belonged for one year to an African American woman who was hired by the president to be the diversity person. Now we have an office of diversity something something something, but his job is mainly with student activities stuff. He brings in speakers and those kinds of things, but she worked with the departments. She got zero support, and then when she went back to the English department

after that one year, there was a commitment from the president's office to hire an outside person to do this job full time. They put out a search, and they brought in candidates, and then nobody was hired. And that's been about three years now. I don't know across the campus what diversity looks like in people's syllabus. Maybe everybody's got a week where they talk about diversity, I don't know—I have no idea. But I think it's an important component to have in everybody's curriculum.

Every once in a while, a conversation could turn almost philosophical, reminding us what a principled disagreement might look like:

> I think there are some senior colleagues who are very suspicious of some of the innovations in that they have taken us away from intellectual work and toward "too much doing." Questions from parents and trustees about the relevance of a liberal arts education are actually questions about meaning. What is the meaning of this education? And we love to talk about meaning in this faculty, but "relevance" gets us all upset. It's like we're insulted. "What do you mean when you're speaking about how relevant or how practical our education is? It's a great education for your child." The response is, "Yeah, I'm paying sixty-five grand a year, though, man, talk to me about the relevance of this." As trustees and parents talk to me about the relevance of this education, I think they're really talking about the "meaning" of our education, and that becomes a really powerful thing that we should love to talk about with them. I think, however, there are some senior faculty who feel like we've gone to relevance rather than meaning.

At other times, the nostrums administrations resort to in order to overcome institutional inertia and faculty intransigency smack of something utilized by a consultant serving as a process coach. One president sought a straw poll that was expected to winnow the options under consideration as part of the strategic planning process. One of the faculty members who had skin in the game, in that his proposal was one of those being considered, picked up the story from there:

> We went into a forum, a faculty forum where the intent was to discuss the six proposals on the floor, and then we were going to take a straw poll to gauge faculty opinion to see where we were. When we all showed up at the forum, and when it came time to take the straw poll, we were told that the straw poll was going to be a binding straw poll as a part of winnowing down the number of alternatives that would be brought forward for consideration.

And so, if you hear folks talk about dropping Hershey's Kisses in mason jars, that refers to the straw poll because that's how we did it. From a legislative behavior standpoint, it was extraordinary; I walked away very . . . let's just put it this way: frustrated.

A colleague continued the story:

That core renewal process to me was clumsy at times. And that was one of the examples where, coming in, I didn't get a sense the faculty were really clear on the question "How do we make this decision about moving in a particular direction?" And I think there was an attempt to kind of not make it so threatening. I think the Hershey's Kiss vote is kind of a straw ballot, and so that was to diminish a little bit of the gravitas of what was at hand. But also I remember at the time thinking we didn't have people on that group who were leading, who were people who either had expertise in voting or measuring people's behavior, measuring people's attitudes or beliefs. So we were kind of doing it in a way, the best we could, without reaching out and getting people with the knowledge and the expertise. That would have helped with the process. And then the straw vote kind of became a binding vote, so it was clumsy. I would say that.

The implied critique of administrative leadership is a thread that runs through many of the narratives we collected. On the other hand, there were fewer who spoke of the challenges of successful leadership in institutions with strong systems of academic governance. A key lesson recounted by one who stepped from a faculty position into an administrative role was simply that there is a lot to learn:

I'm talking about the first year as being like walking through the woods with a blindfold on at night. The second year you took off the blindfold . . . It took probably three years before I really felt like I knew what was going on. I mean, I had plans to do a lot, really fast, and that wasn't going to work. Fortunately, some people got a hold of me and said, "Hey, slow down."

It's the plea to "slow down" that resonates here. While here and there the faculty we spoke with talked about their institution's leadership and the role that the president and other senior administrators played in promoting curricular change, what they mostly did not talk about was faculty leadership—about department chairs or the heads of the faculty senate or council. Rather, what loopiness had bred was a sense of caution, a willingness to seek smaller rather than larger goals, and above all, a willingness to proceed at a deliberate pace that does not venture too far ahead of where the faculty at large live on an issue.

INCENTIVES AND OTHER COMPLICATIONS

An often-repeated plea on the part of the faculty is a call for incentives. If the administration wants changes, it ought to be prepared to pay for them. What we found was that even in the eyes of faculty, incentives had limited effectiveness if they do not occur in a larger institutional framework of support for innovation:

> I am in a group of faculty, sort of like-minded faculty, where we're always poking and saying, "Are there ways we could connect courses? Are there things we could do that would overlap or build synergies?" And it never really gets very far. In fact, I'm going to a lunch today where a bunch of us are going to hammer out ways of connecting our pedagogy and coming up with more innovative structures. But at the end of the day, it is very much of a self-enterprise. The provost's office is good. One of the reasons I overhauled my Political Science 100 course is because there was a two-thousand-dollar grant to fundamentally overhaul an introductory-level course, and that was an incentive for me to do what I was interested in doing anyway. So I pushed it forward, and it's been mildly successful. I didn't have a textbook. I didn't have any sort of guidance on how to do this. I couldn't find anything on my own. And there was no support other than the monetary incentive to help me do it. It's been very much a learning curve for me and the students.

It is an interesting story that developed in a wonderfully revealing way. He started out talking about collaborating with his faculty colleagues and his hopes that they could do something pedagogical together. But there was no traction there. What he did get was a $2,000 special grant from the provost for individually overhauling one course on his own, for which he was grateful but still all alone. And that isolation is compounded because he got the money and nothing else. His new course was a success, but it sent no ripples across the department or the school.

What faculty members most readily affirm, as did the following former associate dean of a major law school, is that "curricular change is a difficult, often unsuccessful endeavor." The changes that succeed are more likely to be revisions than revolutions. She went on to draw a host of important lessons from her experiences changing a law school's curriculum:

> These particular curricular changes were successful because they were good ideas, but also they were worked on. It's a sense of iterating towards

a solution that would be acceptable to those who were gaining, in some sense, and those who were losing, in the sense of how many credits their courses would be, whether their courses would be there. Will the course be required or will it not be required? Will it be one of a set of electives, or will it not be part of that set? Will it be in the first year, or will we have something that's required but that can be taken upper class? What's most important for the students to get early? What should they have before they ever graduate at all? And lots of conversations.

Her testimony gives meaning to the injunction "go slow." Change is more likely to be iterated than enacted. Just as important, her changes leave in place the basic structure of the curriculum and leave undisturbed the notion of individual faculty owning their own courses.

Going slow also means talking more. One of the colleges we visited was in the midst of a reform of its governance structure that included fewer faculty meetings governed by Robert's Rules of Order, including all the special procedures and processes that skilled legislative tacticians have developed to make sure nothing untold ever happens. For that institution, the most important innovation was the convening of smaller discussion groups that were to give everyone a chance to speak. One of our faculty storytellers allowed that the change was successful, but only to a point:

> I think and hope we're doing better. The whole reason faculty council put together the new faculty meeting structure with smaller discussion groups before our large meetings was really meant to foster more conversations. In the huge meetings, the committees present their spiel, and the same, few, brave people stand up and ask questions all the time. I was on leave this fall, and from what I've heard, attendance is not good at these smaller group meetings, but I've spoken to some of the faculty who attend, and they love it. "I actually speak now." So is that a move in the right direction? I don't know. I think it's too soon to know, but I think people are trying for transparency and conversations instead of assuming, "Oh, we're all talking about the same thing."

One more story underscores the importance of talk and commitment to open-ended exchanges. The subject was the new core curriculum the institution was just putting in place:

> What helped the process of developing the new undergraduate core curriculum was having a stick. We really had to do something, but we weren't told, "We have a stick, and it needs to look like this!" The beauty was that we weren't told what to do. Also, I was surprised to be asked to be involved with the whole process, and that maybe contains a few words of

wisdom: don't involve all the usual suspects. It reminds me of one of these thoughts from my community development days. If you always do what you've always done, you're going to always get what you've got.

Anyway, I thought, "What the heck am I being asked to do this for?" I was untenured, not very confident in terms of dealing with tenured people outside my department, and I was asked to be a coleader of one of the groups. I thought, "You've got to be crazy, but all right, I can't say no." There were other unusual suspects in there too, people who were on the younger end of the spectrum or just hadn't been involved with this sort of thing that much. I think that's a really key thing, getting different people involved, getting lots of people involved. You're then tying in all different parts of the campus, getting buy-in from these people, and hopefully using their involvement to pull their resistant colleagues along with them.

Leaving the outcome open was also a key piece of this process. We did research and took best practices and took pieces from here and there, but as long as the program was rooted in the central learning outcomes that the university had already agreed upon, the design was wide open. I think everybody felt the excitement of being able to create something, which was a pretty powerful thing. I think some of the elements of this process can be replicated, whether there's a stick or not.

MOVING ON

We have called this chapter "Barriers" as a way of capturing how faculty members often see the process of curricular change—lots of good ideas but also lots of reasons so few come to fruition. These reasons are the barriers that drain energy, that fracture collectivity, and, in the process, that leave in place the status quo that many, often a majority, of the faculty believe no longer suffices. Some barriers reflect attitudes that were best summed up by the admission that "curricular change is a difficult, often unsuccessful endeavor." Too often the rules get in the way. There is too much minimizing and satisficing behavior. Occasionally it is faculty anger that is the barrier. Sometimes it is the urge to play Whack-a-Mole and thereby silence the naysayers. But mostly, it is the sense of isolation, of being on one's own, of being separate and separated that reduces the prospect of an all-encompassing change.

Another tale of alternative teaching includes elements that would be ideal in most respects—a faculty member beginning a career at a new institution, receiving encouragement from a dean and president to build a program that gives students a distinctive learning experience. The results by any accounting were remarkable, until the foray into experiential learning met the counterforce of tradition, which declared that learning of this kind was not sufficiently rigorous to qualify as higher learning. Still the story ends happily, at least for the moment:

> I went to work for this maverick dean who said to me the first day that I sat down with him, "We're here to make the students' experience better. That's it; that's why we exist. I need you to do that." We also had a brand-new president, and he was interested in civic education, so the dean said to me, "This is kind of interesting; see what you can do with this." I went to the faculty in composition who were my colleagues and said, "Does anybody want to pilot a civic literacies course for the first-year writing course?" There were a couple of people who climbed on board, and we spent six months building this course that we were going to run in the fall. We were all going to teach it, and it was going to be a contemporary look at civic issues.
>
> Then one of my codesigners said one day in another colleague's back-yard, "Why will students want to take this course?" And this is the question that changed my life, and it is how I start with everything now. We decided to embed a town hall meeting in the first-year writing course to give students a purpose beyond the classroom for their writing. The idea was that they would do all the research and writing they would usually do, but it would prepare them to have public dialogues. So we built this thing with about 120 students across these several sections. I then got faculty and administrators to show up to interact with the students. The students were grouped according to research interests about current public issues. They could pick anything, but it had to be a current issue of concern. We ran this town hall as a culminating experience on a Saturday morning near the end of the semester with about 180 people. It was lumpy and weird the way these things are. I couldn't make coffee, and the electricity wouldn't work, but it was electrifying. We had a plenary, and then the students went to breakout sessions where they talked with faculty and administrators about the work they'd been doing. They came back together—and there was this buzz—where we gave them lunch. I was moving around the room during lunch, and they couldn't quit talking about their research. And I said to my colleague, "No matter what, we're doing this."
>
> The next year the dean went after a grant from Bringing Theory to Practice through AAC&U [Association of American Colleges and Universities]. We got that, which helped us with the town hall for two years. There was then a year break, and then I wrote a grant, and AAC&U helped us for another two. The town hall grew to three hundred students the

next semester because faculty saw it, and they wanted to do it. The next semester it was seven hundred students. I kept saying to the undergraduate dean, "We need a plan B, because the people in the English department are going to figure out how to kill this." And they did; they did in spite of these amazing assessments that showed that students were more academically engaged, more civically engaged because they participated in this thing. The English department didn't care. We saw the problem coming, however, and took the town hall over to the department of political science, and they adopted it. So there's never been a break.

One way to surmount the barriers is simply to tone down the tactics intended to protect one's own turf and discipline, to transcend the fixation on "my students," to engage in dialogue characterized by listening as well as speaking, and to focus on what is best for the whole education students receive during their college years. There are glimpses of such behaviors in stories throughout this book, and they can offer instructive principles to guide others.

Faculty Voice

For almost three decades, this professor had been a research scientist and teacher at a major university. Changes in society and in the state of knowledge had led his university to combine a set of departments within his college. Even though the changes would not affect his compensation or standing within his own field, he realized that the process of reconfiguration would have a substantial impact on many of his colleagues. He also understood that if the process were not handled well, it would have lasting consequences for the whole college to which this department belonged. Here he tells the story of assuming a leadership role that he had never imagined would be his until the moment arrived.

I was not looking to be an associate dean, but I've always had a very passionate interest around undergraduate education. The dean at that time grabbed me and asked me to apply, and I said, "No, I don't think so." And he said, "Well, go talk to your wife." And my wife basically said, "Step up to the plate and do this because otherwise I'm going to listen to you complain for the next five years." I think that was probably pretty good advice. I thought about it and looked at it, and from my perspective, there was a window. We had just put two colleges together and were in the process of trying to figure out what the curriculum was going to look like. This was not going to be an opportunity that would probably be there in two or three years. I guess I looked at it as "OK, this is something I'd really be interested in doing."

I went ahead, moved into the associate dean position, and found out within the first six months I didn't know much about how to lead something like this. I made several pretty big mistakes in terms of trying to do something much more top-down rather than involving the faculty. Fortunately, it wasn't that big a deal. I kind of took my bumps and went through several leadership activities, which helped to some extent. And then we launched an initiative to try to revise the curriculum within the college, basically from top to bottom.

This revision was one of those things that I had some ideas about, things I sort of wanted to see happen. By this time, I did realize, "OK, I was a faculty

member, so how would I think about this guy doing this?" I got back around
to very seriously involving the faculty in the whole process.

There were two areas that we focused on. One was that we had a set of
majors that were probably put together fifty years ago, and during that period
of time, there had been major changes in the demographics of the students
and their interests. We tried to make this data driven as much as possible, so
it wasn't "Oh, this is a good idea." We looked at thirty years of data, and I
mean, things had completely shifted. We went from like 10 percent women
to 66 percent women. Mostly suburban and urban now compared to mostly
rural thirty years ago.

So it was a very big change, and it was pretty clear that some of the majors
really just had nobody in them. We sort of thought, "Well, that's a no-brainer.
There are three here that we just need to get rid of." So we made that suggestion, and the pushback was absolutely amazing.

The reasoning that groups of faculty came up with for trying to keep a
major that had one student per year, and we had to listen to those and had to
be very . . . and, you know, it became pretty clear that we needed to back up
and do this in a much more comprehensive manner.

We started with the data collection, and the first thing we wanted was
feedback from students, so we conducted a series of eight listening sessions.
We stratified it by major, and we stratified it by freshman, sophomore, junior,
and senior. We asked them a series of questions about the curriculum, basically
what's working, what's not working, what they'd like to see changed. I had a
staff member that transcribed all those so that we could pass them out to faculty when we got to that point. So that was one of the data-collection pieces,
because you have to realize that we're all scientists in our college. We're driven
by facts, and that's what you know people wanted to see.

We then did similar listening sessions with potential employers of our
students. We spoke with people from state agencies that hire our students,
large employers, and other employers as well. We had a series of questions:
What would you like to see in students you don't see now? Just those types
of questions.

We ended up with a huge amount of data. To be honest, trying to figure
out what to do with all that was a bit of a challenge, but we were able to
pull out themes. We had faculty involved in that process. Partly I wanted faculty to hear it from the mouths of students and also from the mouths of people
in industry, so it wasn't just this thing. The bottom line, I felt that my job was
to lay out some direction, provide resources, and try to energize a bunch of
faculty. I read the book *The Tipping Point* that talks about how you don't need
51 percent of the people to make something happen. You need 10 percent of
the right people. And boy, I think there's an awful lot of truth to that.

I went to the leaders of undergraduate education in all the different academic departments, and we put together a committee that drove this whole process. If you look at our faculty and divide them up into certain groups, there were the innovators out there. That was the 10 percent that I was really trying to work with, because when undergraduate issues came up, everybody looked to those people in the dynamics of department meetings. So I wanted to have all those people in the same room. And it was a fantastic group of people. I really enjoyed working with them.

And at the other far end, there was a group of people trying to get me fired. Like literally. They were very adamant about it. Then there was a big group of people in the middle, and I think the analogy that I used was that they're kind of sitting in the foxholes waiting to see what happens. If it sways this way, they're going to do that; if it sways that way, you know they're going to do this. I tried to be very aware of these dynamics. We did try to include people in different capacities; we didn't have all the top 10 percent because I thought that might be difficult when we got to the tough part.

We had two committees. We had this one committee that dealt with restructuring the curriculum and then another one thinking about where we could move the curriculum forward, not just structurally, but in terms of questions like, What are we missing? What are we hearing from the employers and from the students? This committee's work was clear. We needed to do experiential learning and be more interdisciplinary. The other committee dealt with changing the majors. What are our students and employers looking for that we do not have or is packaged in a different way? What really needs to go away? It actually was very clear from the data what those answers were, but it was with this committee where I really had some challenges.

What worked? Well, I'll tell you about one of our majors that had been declining significantly over the last several years. It was also an area we need to have. We didn't really want to do away with it, but we wanted to combine it with another major because there is a lot of overlap, and it just made sense to do that. So I kind of laid that out. And then the other thing was that we needed a new major that dealt with emerging fields of interest in the sciences. The idea was to have this be lateral across several disciplines rather than very reductionist, like most of our disciplines tend to be.

So there's a fellow in one of the affected departments, and he is clearly a leader of what goes on in that department. He came to me and told me what a horrible idea this was and that we absolutely couldn't do this; the industry wasn't going to go for it. I said, "OK," and we kind of kept going. I've really got to give this guy credit. He listened to his faculty, he looked at the data we had, he talked to his people. A year later, he was actually the person who led the change because what he came back with and what he told me was, "I had to realize that I'm not doing this for me. I'm five to ten years from retirement. I'm doing it for the new faculty and our students." And when he went and talked to them, the message he got was, "Yeah, this is the direction that we ought to go." Once it was his idea, I just kind of stood back and watched him go.

That experience gave me a lot of perspective as to what my role should be. I threw out ideas. Some of them stuck; some of them didn't. But everything had to go through a process of vetting by the faculty.

When I took the job, I said, "Three years, that's it. I want to get back to my faculty position; I'm going to do this for three years." It was seven. After three years, we had just started having serious discussions around it. I was amazed how slow it went for a group of people who are incredibly creative in their research and in their teaching. Trying to come up with these changes was excruciating for everybody. I mean, this was not a simple process. I don't want to have it come across that way, and there were certainly days that I thought, "I'm done; I'm going to go back to the faculty." I told myself, as long as there were at least three days during the week that I thought this was going well, I'd stay with it. And there were only a couple of weeks that went, you know, the other way.

PART FIVE

Conclusions

CHAPTER 8

The Road Not Traveled

WE HAVE COME FULL circle. Traveling across the country, visiting eleven different institutions, talking with more than 180 individual faculty members both confirmed what we had always known and, at the same time, taught us about elements of faculty life we had never considered. We have learned much about how faculty view their worlds—and were often impressed by the intense commitment embedded in their calling as teachers. Most often, they had a passion that derived from the satisfaction found not just in contributing to but in actually shaping their students' learning. What they sought as faculty members were learning environments that prepared their students for the many futures they envisioned.

Just as important to the faculty was the energy that came from a life committed to continued growth, one that both sustained their habits of inquiry and discovery and validated the meaning and relevance of their scholarship. They defined as essential the academic independence that encourages the pursuit of knowledge and expression of thought without constraint. It is an independence that allows individual faculty members to design their own courses, to teach as they think best, and to determine, with minimal constraints, the content of the courses that they believe they own.

Their passions do not come without costs. The very independence they celebrate makes it nearly impossible to change the curriculum. Metrics are often viewed as unnecessary intrusions—something to be put up with as the price of accreditation rather than as subjects for fruitful conversation. Most of these faculty members, it turned out, had little understanding of the relationship between how and what they taught, on the one hand, and institutional revenues and expenditures, on the other. Like the public at large, they were increasingly concerned about the growing cost of earning a college degree and the impact rising tuitions have on the diversity of the student body. Some worried that higher education may be doing more to exacerbate than to reduce the divide between the educational "haves" and "have-nots." And yet very few faculty we met felt empowered to help reverse the trend. This challenge registered as one that was beyond their ability—or even the ability of their institution—to solve alone.

In their stories, they frequently confessed to not having any real appreciation for what it means to participate in organizational decision-making. They often talked about lacking sufficient experience to affirm and follow decisions made through a collective process. While most of the faculty whose stories we collected had a finely calibrated sense of the obstacles they faced, when seeking to change how and what they taught, they also admitted to not knowing how to navigate organizational barriers that were mostly of their own making. Their stories also demonstrated just how different their views about pedagogical methods could be. In often the same passage, they embraced the tenants of experiential learning while remembering to celebrate the traditional virtues of the lecture or class discussion but also voiced caution, and sometimes outright skepticism, about the use of technology as a tool to enhance the learning process. In much the same vein, faculty members readily talked about their interest in and practice of interdisciplinary work. Among the stories we collected, however, the instances of collaborative work and teaching were comparatively few.

The same yin and yang often characterized these faculty members' sense of their students. They see the students of the current generation presenting greater challenges than their forbearers. Students' preoccupations with digital technology and social media present particular challenges in motivating students to learn—or simply commanding their attention. Too often students are shoppers rather than learners, more likely to pursue pathways that promise specific jobs rather than pathways that promote sustained learning. And yet much more than among past generations of faculty, those whose stories we collected were prepared to take and teach their students as they came to them rather than lamenting that their students were not prepared to learn what a college education ought to teach them.

RESOLVING OUR RIDDLE

Understanding this faculty persona is the first step to resolving the riddle that lies at the heart of this volume. Why has there not been more sustainable curricular reform across American higher education? The answer is not that the faculty resist change. Quite the contrary. American higher education has changed dramatically in the three decades since the publication of *A Nation at Risk* and then *Integrity in the College Curriculum.* Total enrollments in undergraduate institutions have increased by 60 percent, growing from 10.8 million in 1982 to 17.4 million in 2016. That enrollment is significantly more heterogeneous than in the 1980s—more people of color, more older learners, more global students, individuals more varied in terms of their families' incomes and their individual financial prospects.

The institutions that serve these students have changed as well, becoming more complex, more enterprise-like, and more market savvy. Where there were but a handful of for-profit institutions thirty-five years ago—for the most part family-owned businesses—today the for-profit sector accounts for 10 percent of all undergraduate enrollments and nearly a third of the political attention higher education attracts. The big universities have gotten bigger. The most prestigious among them benefit from a new abundance of applications for what remains a remarkably limited number of places in their first-year classes. Today, there are fewer classical liberal arts colleges, as the market for an undergraduate education has shifted, largely in response to the job anxieties of students and parents.

Faculty demographics have changed as well. While the traditional notion of the scholar-teacher armed with a PhD continues to hold sway, the truth of the matter is that today's undergraduates are increasingly being taught by someone else—an adjunct, either full time or part time, who is less connected to his or her employing institution and, as a consequence, less a part of the lives of the undergraduates they teach. Faculty of every stripe are more likely to see themselves as being interdisciplinary in their research and teaching even as they have become ever more specialized.

There have been equally dramatic shifts in the content being taught across colleges and universities. The knowledge base itself has expanded, often geometrically. New majors as well as new disciplines abound. There have been changes in the basic topology of the industry. The nation's community colleges, now accounting for upwards of 40 percent of all enrollments, have developed whole new sets of products, ranging from vocational certificates to vocationally defined baccalaureate degrees, meant to serve an ever-changing labor market.

The most dramatic but ironically the least celebrated changes have been in how faculty teach. What has transpired over the last thirty-five years is nothing short of a pedagogical revolution. If, as our stories observed, a more muted sage on the stage remains, most faculty today are more guides than savants, more mentors and interpreters than truth tellers or arbiters. That commitment to active learning and student engagement is broad and enduring. Internships are necessities. Flipped classrooms with or without clickers can be found everywhere. If the MOOC revolution proved somewhat less than overwhelming, the idea that the new technologies will change both teachers and those who are taught is taken today as a given. Learning management systems are standard means of organizing and tracking learning experiences.

While most faculty remain leery of externally imposed systems for assessing student learning, there is a begrudging sense that assessment is something that the faculty will have to take much more seriously in the future. Programs of general education that were principally enrollment allocation systems, distributing student places among the competing departments, have begun to morph into minicurricula, sometimes with logics and processes of their own.

Why then, to repeat our riddle, has there been so little curricular change despite all these demographic, institutional, and pedagogical upheavals? Why do student transcripts resemble menu cards for the kind of learning smorgasbords that *Integrity in the College Curriculum* inveighed against so vehemently? Why are the three-credit course and the four-year degree still the standards almost everywhere? Why have assessment and accreditation proved to be such weak prods in the struggle to make an undergraduate education more affordable?

Framed in this manner, our riddle poses what can best be described as a Frostian moment. Why pedagogical and not curricular change? Sometime over the last thirty years, American higher education made a choice to pursue the former and not the latter. Part of the answer lies in the extraordinary success of the movement sustained by the Association of American Colleges and Universities (AAC&U). Carol Geary Schneider, a gifted historian turned educational innovator, transformed a quiet organization, lodged in an old town house on R Street in the nation's capital, into a national platform for promoting pedagogical change. Its conferences, its gift for aptly named slogans—LEAP (Liberal Education and America's Promise) being the prime example—its workshops promoting practical means that carried the promise of more effective teaching all contributed to the promotion of active learning and student engagement.

AAC&U's organizational success, however, is only part of the answer. What Schneider, LEAP, and a growing catalog of innovative programs took advantage of was the fact that pedagogical change was largely an individual response to the altered circumstances faculty were encountering everywhere. It was the kind of change that did not challenge the faculty member's personal control of what was taught, when, where, or how. Change remained individualistic—a matter of what I do in my classroom. One seldom, if ever, needed to ask permission of someone else in order to change how one taught. Pedagogical change not only left intact but actually reinforced the individual faculty member's sense of personal space and independence, of self and personal success.

What we are suggesting then is that sometime in the last thirty years, there really was a moment when higher education chose, though never quite consciously, the other road, the one easier to travel, always promising itself that it could come back later to the challenge of curricular reform, though it never did. While it is the first stanza of Robert Frost's "The Road Not Taken" that is most often recalled, from our perspective, it is the third stanza that contains the kernel of truth we have been pursuing:

> And both that morning equally lay
> In leaves no step had trodden black.
> Oh, I kept the first for another day!
> Yet knowing how way leads on to way,
> I doubted if I should ever come back.

What our story collecting has taught us is simple enough to summarize. Curricular change is really tough, for lots of reasons. Curricular change, unlike pedagogical innovation, requires collective action. A whole system has to be changed, often in its entirety. Everyone must adapt to the new rules, including all those folks not at all certain that change is either necessary or desirable. Three of the institutions at which we collected faculty stories had experimented with curricular changes that impacted everyone—and each, in the end, discovered something of a mixed lesson. The first had adopted a truly revolutionary general education program filled with new courses that were both linked and substantive rather than just being recruiting platforms for departments in search of majors. Three years later, however, much of the ardor had cooled. The initiative's leader had departed for another campus in a neighboring state. The popular provost who had promoted the curricular change was passed over in favor of another candidate for president. And the politics of the state had further soured the campus climate. The new gen ed curriculum survived, but just barely, and no one was talking about extending the lessons learned to the campus's general curriculum or its majors.

We also visited a humanities department that had undergone a major revision of its major. A whole new schema of courses had been put in place, and at the same time, the department embraced team teaching as a principal mode of instruction. Ultimately, the department discovered it simply didn't have enough faculty resources to teach the new curriculum. Buyer's remorse had set in, leaving everyone both edgy and confused.

A third example is a nearly twenty-year experiment with a fundamentally new curriculum at a private comprehensive university. We have already presented the story of the funeral this university had for its old curriculum, and while the result has been a more coherent curriculum in support of core learning goals, the effort had not succeeded in reducing costs or achieving another desired result—a badly needed uptick in undergraduate enrollments.

There are rules governing teaching loads, allotting credit for the teaching of single courses, jointly taught courses, seminars, laboratory sessions, even field trips. There are rules defining how many credits a major can require, whether other majors or courses can be linked to programs outside the department responsible for offering a specific major, and, with the growing focus on assessment, how faculty are expected to document their students' learning. With rules come processes and procedures defining how the rules are to be either adopted or changed: who has a vote, what agency or individual has final approval how far in advance a change has to be proposed, and what kinds of assessments will be used to evaluate the change once it is implemented. It is this intertwining of rules, procedures, and processes that nearly everywhere became the focus of stories documenting the barriers and frustrations that faculty seeking curricular change felt too often blocked their way.

Then there is the fact that the faculty members often do not understand how rules translate into the dollars that are associated with academic activity in general and the curriculum in particular. We were surprised by how little the faculty with whom we spoke understood the economics of their institutions and their readiness to admit they knew too little. One of the major changes across higher education over the last three decades has been the conversion of colleges and universities of nearly every size and stripe into what, in fact, are business enterprises governed by budget systems that have real winners and losers. Most faculty don't understand how these systems work, how they allocate resources, or why, if you push in here, something is likely to squeeze out over there.

On top of all these barriers and obstacles, there are the traditions and habits of mind that define the faculty persona. The quest for autonomy, the wish to be beholden to no one, and the sense of owning one's own teaching space—my teaching, my students, my room—all serve to increase resistance to the kind of system-wide, all-embracing change that recasting a collegiate curriculum requires. Despite—though more likely because of—the myriad rules and procedures etched into faculty governance processes, it is seldom if ever possible to compel faculty behavior. The establishment of codified research rules managed by functioning institutional review boards (IRBs) is an exception, but nothing like these bodies exists to provide either oversight or compliance on how, what, when, or where faculty teach their courses. Simply to suggest a possible mandate providing broad advice on curricular issues is to invite a vehement appeal to the sanctity of academic freedom.

If the choice facing would-be faculty innovators is between pursuing a program of curricular as opposed to pedagogical change, the latter wins almost every time. Pedagogical change is most often small scale, involving a limited number of faculty pursuing interests of their own. As long as the faculty member is being supported in his or her efforts to teach differently, there is no abridgment of another member's sense of his or her independence. Indeed, it is the freedom to teach as the individual faculty member prefers that makes the pursuit of pedagogical reform so attractive.

Its scale also makes pedagogical reform less expensive and the cost of failure almost negligible. Changing a handful of courses, for the most part, one course at a time is relatively simple. Even when summer or other stipends are involved, the number receiving those funds at any one time is relatively limited. Failures are also less costly—for the most part, they can be simply abandoned with a minimum of fuss and bother.

Nor must individual programs of pedagogical innovation form a coherent whole. What one group of faculty does need not limit what other faculty may want to do. Often the most successful campaigns promoting pedagogical change celebrate the diversity of programs that let a thousand blossoms bloom.

Launching a program of curricular reform is inherently more difficult. Genuine curricular reform is almost always large scale, involving everybody. Whole faculties must be cajoled into endorsing a proposed change as being in their own best interest.

Curricular reform is also inherently expensive, even when the reform involves but a single department. Those who push campaigns of curricular reform must be prepared to flatter everyone; broadly distribute incentives, both monetary and otherwise; and threaten vested interests in near equal measure. Curricular reform involves not just one or even a group of courses but nearly the full catalog of offerings, depending on how extensive a reform is being sought. When the new curriculum requires new courses, and it almost always does, start-up time and monies are required, often in large amounts.

At the same time, failure cannot be an option—and in that sense, curricular reform is fundamentally more risky than pedagogical innovation. In the latter, an abandoned experiment is quickly forgotten—as in the case of the MOOCs that many campuses tried without much success. When it is the curriculum that is being changed, the solution to the problem the new curriculum is expected to address becomes locked in. Recall our earlier examples of institutions that found out, only after fully implementing a new curriculum, that the changes proved much more expensive than anticipated and were replete with unintended consequences.

There are two final differences that are worth noting. Pedagogical change is almost always an exercise in addition—the new, improved courses are simply added to the curriculum. Curricular reform, on the other hand, is almost always about subtraction, reflecting the reforming faculty's conviction that there are too many unconnected courses, too many majors and minors, too many opportunities for students to get lost in a maze of choices that they don't really understand. That was certainly the opinion of the authors of *Integrity in the College Curriculum*. The problem, as the faculty whose stories we collected often pointed out, is that faculty bodies almost never subtract, neither substituting nor eliminating that which has proved extraneous.

Finally, curricular reform requires major rule changes; pedagogical change almost never does. The stories we collected are full of examples of proposed curricular changes and innovations that were blocked by the rules governing teaching loads, graduation requirements, and the organization of the major.

CHANGING DIRECTIONS

In April 2017, Judith Shapiro, on behalf of the Teagle Foundation, convened a gathering of faculty and administrators from the colleges that had been awarded Teagle grants to pursue curricular coherence in an age of educational specialization. *Checklist for Change* had played a role in shaping the request for proposals the foundation had issued two years earlier. Bob Zemsky was among the invited guests, both as the author of *Checklist* and as the principal investigator for our Teagle grant that funded the collection of the faculty stories that are the focus of this volume. The first evening of the convening featured an extended conversation between Ann Ferren of AAC&U and Bob, moderated by President Shapiro. Toward the end of the session, Judith asked what was the one thing each discussant would recommend that an institution committed to curricular coherence should do. Bob's answer was a little surprising. He suggested that the faculty should be asked to read this book that you are now reading. His reasoning, he went on to explain, was that it was important for the faculty to understand just how tough the challenge they were taking on was—to understand that they were not alone and that what faculty had learned elsewhere could help shape their own efforts for reform.

Bob's brief excursion into self-advertisement was not the first nor, we suspect, the last occasion on which we will be asked, "Well, 'smarty,' what would you do?" As we made our way across the country collecting our stories, we encountered faculty that had been intrigued by the argument presented in *Checklist for Change*—that what was required before plans could be specified and strategies enunciated were more collaborative organizational arrangements that linked members of the faculty to one another across disciplines, programs, and departments. Or as *Checklist* argued, what was required were fewer faculty members who saw themselves as independent agents doing good but for the most part doing good separately and independently.

Now is the time to refine the advice that we originally offered extemporaneously. A campaign for curricular reform necessarily ought to begin with a tough conversation about what needs to happen. And what is being envisioned ought to be something big, like reducing the number of majors, or recasting general education, or developing a three-year, ninety-credit baccalaureate degree. Departments can be asked to refashion their majors, drawing more explicitly on courses taught by other departments. Or the goal might be first to imagine and then implement curricula that include more collaborative teaching, more programs that share faculty members and individual courses, more clear distinctions between introductory and culminating experiences. We are not suggesting that all these goals should be pursued simultaneously— quite the contrary, there needs to be a judicious discussion that allows the identification of just a few, but necessarily difficult, changes that need to be made now.

The next task is to identify the institutional rules, procedures, processes, traditions, and habits of mind that will need to be confronted if the desired reform is to prove sustainable. We cannot stress enough the importance of this step. Read again the stories presented in this volume that describe good starts and bad endings because the rules got in the way—rules that limited the effectiveness of team teaching, or proscribed requirements that protected turf, or mandated schedules that proved intractable.

Only then, we have argued, can effective reform proceed, because curricular change is as much about rule changing as it is about changing what and how students learn. Unless institutions and their faculty are prepared to consider and then adopt new rules for calculating teaching loads, defining majors, and specifying cross-major or cross-disciplinary programs, there is little chance the curricular changes the faculty have in mind will prove either possible or sustainable.

The need to focus on curricular rules was but the first hard lesson we derived from our collection of faculty stories. No less important is the need to seek outside help—skilled facilitators who know how to assist faculty in bringing their deliberations to a successful conclusion. On occasion, we have even laid out a work plan that we thought would get the faculty and institution moving in the right direction. What follows is our sketch of a facilitated process that we think will yield both a better understanding of how an institution's processes, procedures, and organizational arrangements might best be altered to encourage more collaborative endeavors and a series of curricular changes leading to a more efficient and effective undergraduate curriculum. Assuming the process would begin in the summer months, the timeline would extend as follows:

Start-Up Phase
- Appoint a faculty *coordinating committee*, probably best cochaired by two faculty members from different departments from across the institution. This committee would guide the project's discussions and considerations of alternate policies, procedures, and organizational arrangements as well as alternate curricular arrangements.

- In August, convene an all-faculty conversation about the prospects and opportunities for more collaborative faculty strategies and initiatives. It is here the leadership of the initiative needs to describe, in considerable and hopefully precise detail, the kind of curricular changes that are needed.

September

- Convene up to ten faculty work groups charged with considering the kinds of processes, procedures, and organizational arrangements that might prove advantageous. It would be important to link each of these possible organizational changes, encouraging more collaborative faculty endeavors to specific curricular changes and promoting a more efficient and effective curriculum.
- The coordinating committee reviews proposals from individual work groups in order to set the agenda for a second all-faculty conversation in January.

January

- A second all-faculty conversation reviews specific curricular proposals and linked organizational changes as put forward by the coordinating committee.
- Faculty work groups review and comment on results of the all-faculty conversation.

March

- A third all-faculty conversation begins the formal process for considering changes to faculty processes, policy, and organizational arrangements.
- Work groups recommend specific changes to the college's curriculum.
- The coordinating committee uses work group recommendations to develop a final proposal-defining rule and curricular changes.

August

- A fourth all-faculty conversation convenes to consider and approve revised curriculum and rule changes.

We know that our proposed way of proceeding is expensive, both in terms of faculty time and what it would cost to engage the team of facilitators. What is being proposed is an extended process of reverse engineering. Define the end that is being sought. Work backward to identify the processes and obstacles that must be addressed. Then and only then, design the new curricular arrangements that will be put in place.

Many of the stories the faculty told us were frustrating narratives of failure—of good ideas and goodwill floundering in the end. We remain convinced, however, of the soundness of the two basic lessons Bob shared that night with the leaders of the institutions attending the Teagle convening. Our answer to the question "Can there be curricular change?" is "Yes, if you—as an institution and as a faculty—are tough and resolute enough." What is required in the first instance are new work rules. There needs to be a demonstrably greater commitment to collaborative work; faculty groups need to see themselves more like cooperatives and collectives and less like convenings of independent instructors, each owning his or her own classroom and each the only arbiter of what, when, and how he or she teaches. The kinds of rules we have in mind are those that promote shared responsibility and collaborative behavior.

Our second concluding lesson is that faculty will need help coming to this conclusion. At several of the institutions we visited, we suggested that help could best come in the form of facilitation, preferably by men and women who were themselves faculty but who came from somewhere else. As the stories we collected make clear, faculty are fully aware of how special interests divide them. The role of the facilitator is to help them find common ground, moving away from debates about winners and losers and instead convening conversations that are student focused and thereafter cognizant of why it is that the faculty have come to the academy and stayed. The advantage of facilitation suggests that what is also needed are programs of purposeful training to help faculty talk through those habits that too often divide them.

LOST IN THE WOODS AGAIN

On more than one occasion, faculty confessed to being less than perfect partners in the sense of not playing well together. Toward the end of the drafting of this volume, the three of us came to realize that we were each thinking of the same image, though initially we could neither place nor remember it. An hour spent exploring word associations and then a quick Google search led us to what we hadn't been able to recall: an old Walt Kelly *Pogo* cartoon, which found Kelly's eponymous hero and his buddy Porkypine in the woods confronting mounds of trash everywhere. Published on the second Earth Day in 1971, the cartoon has Pogo drawing the lesson that matters most: "We have met the enemy and he is us."

We began by reminding ourselves that storytelling was about survival. We tell stories so that we can sort through the rough of our lives. The enduring lessons are those that testify as to what is important and worth preserving. We know that *Pogo*'s lesson bears repeating. If we can't reform the curriculum together—collectively, cooperatively, completely—then we can't do it at all.

References

AAC (Association of American Colleges). 1985. *Integrity in the College Curriculum: A Report to the Academic Community.* Washington, D.C.: Association of American Colleges.

Bok, Derek. 2008. *Our Underachieving Colleges: A Candid Look at How Much Students Learn and Why They Should Be Learning More.* Princeton, N.J.: Princeton University Press.

Delistraty, Cody C. 2014. "The Psychological Comforts of Storytelling: Why, Throughout Human History, Have People Been So Drawn to Fiction?" *The Atlantic,* November 2. https://www.theatlantic.com/health/archive/2014/11/the-psychological-comforts -of-storytelling/381964/.

Fisher, Roger, and William Ury. 1981. *Getting to Yes: Negotiating Agreement without Giving In.* Boston, Mass.: Houghton Mifflin.

National Commission on Excellence in Education. 1983. *A Nation at Risk: The Imperative for Educational Reform.* A Report to the Nation and the Secretary of Education, United States Department of Education, April. Washington, D.C.: U.S. Department of Education.

Zemsky, Robert. 2013. *Checklist for Change: Making American Higher Education a Sustainable Enterprise.* New Brunswick, N.J.: Rutgers University Press.

Index

About the Authors

ROBERT ZEMSKY currently serves as chair of the Learning Alliance and was a member of the U.S. Secretary of Education's *Commission on the Future of Higher Education*. He is the author of several books, including *Checklist for Change: Making American Higher Education a Sustainable Enterprise*.

After earning a PhD in English in the mid-1980s, GREGORY R. WEGNER became involved in several projects to affirm the ability of colleges and universities to fulfill their education and research missions and sustain the public trust. He was associate director of Penn's Institute for Research on Higher Education for some fifteen years before becoming director of program development for the Great Lakes Colleges Association, a consortium of thirteen liberal arts colleges in four Midwestern states. In that role, he has helped launch several consortial programs that contribute to the professional development of faculty members in all academic fields.

ANN J. DUFFIELD is a strategic planning and communications consultant to colleges and universities and serves on the board of trustees of the Sage Colleges in Troy and Albany, New York. She spent twenty-six years at the University of Pennsylvania (1973-2000) during which time she was the university's and university medical center's chief communications officer and ultimately head of communications for Penn's Institute for Research on Higher Education. In 2000, Ann joined the fundraising consulting firm of Marts & Lundy both to establish and head a new practice in communications and planning and to learn the "art" of consulting. In 2005, she established a practice to provide strategic counsel, focusing on the challenges confronting American higher education, to administrative and academic leaders at liberal arts colleges and public universities.